EGO IN A TEABAG

HOW GREED, CORRUPTION AND DECEIT THREATEN A GREAT AMERICAN MOVEMENT

Ego In a Tea Bag:

How Greed, Corruption and Deceit Threaten A Great American Movement

ISBN-13: 978-1985408319
ISBN-10: 1985408317

Book Design by Logotecture

crowsnestpolitics.com

First Edition

Published by Daria Anne DiGiovanni, LLC

Printed in the U.S.A.

CONTENTS

EGO IN A TEABAG

HOW GREED, CORRUPTION AND DECEIT THREATEN A GREAT AMERICAN MOVEMENT

KEN CROW

ACKNOWLEDGMENTS

A heartfelt thank you to my wife, Sonya Jean, and my mother for believing in me and pushing me into this next chapter of my life. Your encouragement and love are ever sustaining and appreciated.

Charlie, without you, none of this would have been possible. You're truly a gentleman's gentleman and a wonderful friend.

Lisa and Daria, I simply don't have the words to describe how grateful I am to the both of you and the gang at Writestream Publishing. I shall always be humbled and grateful that you were willing to walk on hot coals for me.

To Karen Dianne, I owe you beyond measure. You're the truest definition of a friend and have been there for me for the duration of my lifetime journey. Who would have ever thought we would be here today, back when I rode my little scooter to your home on Lake Heights so very long ago? Had you told me back then about today, I would have laughed at you. Hugs and love to my oldest and dearest friend.

To Tim and Michelle, the tears, the laughter, the pain, and the conversation have all been worth it. Between your vision and brilliance and my tenacity, we did it. We might not have accomplished everything we wanted, but we sure came a long way. Thank you for the friendship, love, and support.

My friends Ralph and Ken, your political wisdom has been cherished and I cannot begin to thank the both of you enough. You taught me so much and I have listened to every word. Besides being like Yoda to me, the both of you took me under your wings and taught me more than you know.

To Terry, if everyone in this world had a friend like you, the world would be a much better place. I honestly don't have the words. It is an honor to call you "friend."

To Valley Mills Independent School District in Texas, although I did not complete 12 years at your schools, I did attend long enough to learn from the best. My seventh grade English teacher Mrs. Wilson taught me about nouns and verbs, how to write and structure a sentence, and to sit straight in my chair. Mr. Mingus taught me about life while teaching me FFA. Thanks to his mentoring on my steer, I learned about respect, developed a love for wildlife and animals, and cultivated patience – all while finding refuge from a rough situation. Coach Robinson taught me to suck it up and be tough when needed. From him I learned the value of perseverance and how to emerge a winner in the face of adversity. I have carried these traits with me for my entire life; you will never know the depth of my gratitude for the education I received, which encompassed so much more than just book knowledge.

ONE

AND SO IT BEGINS

February 19, 2009 began like any other day in Chicago. Rick Santelli, the Chicago Stock Exchange reporter for CNBC, arrived for another day on the job. Events quickly began changing when he got to the floor and witnessed the rising anger of traders and the American people. Santelli began feeling the same rage toward President Barack Obama's economic policies as most everyone else (on the right side of the aisle) did that day.

Just 24 hours before, the President had signed into law the now infamous *Homeowners Affordability and Stability Plan* (HASP). HASP infused $75 billion of America's tax dollars into helping struggling families stay in their homes. The bill went further in that it paid $200 billion dollars to what we now know as a corrupt and floundering Fannie Mae and Freddie Mac.

Keep in mind that all of this was on the heels of the $700 billion that had been paid out by then-President George W. Bush for a TARP (Troubled Asset Relief Program). This was spent to keep the major banks from sending America back into a Great Depression – or so everyone thought at the time.

In a span of just a little over five months, America had added some $1 trillion dollars to our national debt. Not only was Rick Santelli angry, he was livid. Not only at the government for guaranteeing the mortgages in the first place, but also the borrowers for taking out home loans they couldn't afford. There was no question about it: America was headed into an economic tailspin and Santelli was about to voice his anger.

When the cameras turned to Santelli and the light went green, he began what is now known as the *Santelli Rant*. Standing behind him at their respective desk and computers were dozens of brokers and other employees. As Santelli launched into his tirade against the President, he was met with cheers and shouts of approval from those in attendance. It was then the infamous words escaped his lips. *I think I will form another Tea Party and call it the Chicago Tea Party*! He went on to say he would not only form a Tea Party but would hold a rally in Chicago. In the conservative grassroots movement across America known as the Tea Party, those words would live in infamy.

Out on the snow-covered fields of Iowa, there was another fellow listening to the frustration that Santelli was ushering forth from the floor of the Stock Exchange. Santelli might have thought he was just speaking for himself that day, but in reality, he actually gave voice to millions of angry Americans.

Charlie Gruschow was not only listening, he was also caught up in the anger. Santelli was speaking and expressing Charlie's thoughts and passions. The more Santelli talked, the angrier and more frustrated Charlie became. When Santelli mentioned the now famous Chicago Tea Party verbiage, Charlie immediately thought: why not Des Moines also? By April 15, 2009, Charlie and a band of trusted Patriots had not only formed the Des Moines Tea Party, but they also held their first rally (protest) on the steps of the Iowa State Capitol. The magic date of April 15 is not really that complicated to understand; it's the date that resonates with Americans everywhere, when most of them are forced to write checks to the federal government. If one is starting a new movement of campaigning against government waste and frivolous spending, what better date to hold a major protest than April 15?

But Charlie and the thousands who showed up to join him on the steps of the Iowa Capitol on April 15, 2009 were not alone. Along with the Des Moines event, protests were being held in many more cities across America almost at the same time. Hartford, Connecticut, and Atlanta, Georgia were two of the largest. It is estimated that some 346 cities and communities held a protest, with an estimated 318,000 people attending those first tax day protests after Santelli's speech. Many of the smaller events had only dozens protesting while Atlanta and Hartford had numbers in excess of ten-thousand.

These first formal protests and rallies seemed to be spurred by sheer anger directed at Barack Obama and his new way of governing. Obama had not only bailed out Fannie Mae and Freddie Mac, but he was now talking about the auto industry and their struggles, in addition to his future health care initiatives. The protesters could see the handwriting on the wall in with respect to ever-expanding and more intrusive government.

While the first protests were certainly directed at the Obama Administration's "dumping" of some $275 billion to "bail out" – what the Tea Party regarded as bad policy – the shouts of anger did not end with just wasteful spending. The protests grew to include Constitutional subject matter too, with copies of The Bill of Rights and Constitution handed out at rallies where speakers addressed the crowds on the topic of Constitutional Law. Steve McCoy from Indianola, Iowa, a.k.a. Patrick Henry, often attends the Des Moines rallies and gives constitutional lessons to eager attendees.

By April the 15, there was precious little doubt that hundreds of thousands of Americans now viewed the new President and his Administration with disdain and as an enemy of the state. Many new Patriots (as they like to be called), rightly or wrongly, were now convinced that the Obama Administration was not only governing in an amateurish manner, but might possibly be gearing up to seize control of America as a whole.

On the same day Charlie was putting together the Des Moines Tea Party, down in Georgia, a lady had the exact same thought – except on an expanded scale. Jenny Beth Martin and her husband had just seen their home go into foreclosure and they too were seeing red with frustration and anger. Jenny Beth claims she was angry; she did not want Obama's money and believed the policy of writing checks to bail out some 8-10 million Americans mortgages was bad for the country. This thought process fueled the Martins' rage and give birth to the *Tea Party Plank*, if you will. The April 15 protest that had gripped America and had the nightly newscasters wondering, "what is going on?" was raw and unscripted in nature. Martin and many others would come to the conclusion that the Tea Party needed a little bit of direction and something solid to stand on.

Jenny Beth teamed up with a cowboy/attorney from California by the name of Mark Meckler and flight attendant Amy Kremer to form *Tea Party Patriots*. Tea Party Patriots not only had a nice, patriotic ring to it, but the organization was the first to encompass all of America. Its goal was to form a national headquarters in Georgia, then set up separate Tea Party Patriots branches in each state. These branches would be utilized to take the fight as they saw it to each individual state in an effort to fulfill the truest definition of a *grassroots* organization.

Almost at the same moment in time when Charlie was organizing in Iowa and Jenny Beth was hard at work in Georgia, Lisa Feroli got to work in Orlando, Florida. She had posted a public email complaining about all the stimulus spending, which had been picked up by a local talk radio host. After reading the email on the air to his vast listening audience, Lisa received thousands of emails from conservatives wanting to protest. Whether Lisa wanted to be a Tea Party leader or not is up for question, but nevertheless, she became one. She too, organized a mass protest for April, 15. Since that rather awkward inception of the Orlando Tea Party, the good patriots of Central Florida have seen their organization develop into one of the largest in America.

The results of the success of the first Orlando rally of over 5,000 angry Patriots were quite stunning. Not long after that first rally in April of 2009, about 150 Tea Party groups sprung up across the Sunshine State. In fact, the sheer number of groups and members demanded the creation of a website just to handle the inquiries from thousands of Florida citizens who wanted to know where they could find a local organization in their area.

After the smoke had cleared from the hundreds of Tax Day rallies across America, it was then that Jenny Beth's partner Mark Meckler and the rest of the Patriots' upper-crust saw an incredible marketing opportunity. Meckler has a history of involvement in network marketing, having been an executive with the HerbaLife Corporation. Almost immediately Jenny Beth and Meckler began an online narrative marketing plan to raise money for *The Cause* of liberty and freedom.

Throughout this mass marketing effort, several processes take place. The Patriots not only garner your personal information such as your email address, mailing address, and phone number, they also snag a passionate person who cares deeply about their country. After you have complied with their request, you begin receiving fervent emails because Meckler and company knew how much you cared for your country and feared for its future; otherwise, you would not have joined *The Cause*.

The emails and letters you'd receive would isolate a particular "hot button" item, the theory being if you felt strongly enough about it, you would donate money to assist in the fight. Take one of the biggest areas of interests targeted (if you'll pardon the pun) by Tea Party Patriots: gun rights. Any time the President would address the matter of guns, you could count on getting an email the next day with a dire warning that he was about to seize them from you, and to please donate *right now* to help the Patriots fight this egregious assault on your Second Amendment rights. The Patriots ran with fundraising narratives on anything and everything you can think of. They ran them on oil pipelines, coal mining, green energy, healthcare, foreign diplomacy and the list goes on. All of them would describe a forthcoming emergency with Barack Obama or Nancy Pelosi (Former Speaker of the House) and the exhortation that the only way to save America was to donate to the Patriots who are fighting on your behalf. The tragedy is, they could do nothing.

Word spread far and wide that this organization was in the trenches fighting for liberty and freedom. By the mid-terms of 2010, their membership had grown into the millions. There is much dispute about how many actually joined than how many are actually active. But there is little disputing that the Tea Party Patriots are the largest Tea Party group in America. This dubious honor has to go to Mark Meckler for his incredible marketing and merchandising ability. There is zero speculation that the Patriots have earned millions upon millions of dollars for their efforts.

The question now becomes: *Where has the money gone?*

Remember, Jenny Beth's home was in foreclosure when she helped form the organization; today rumors run rampant that she now owns several houses and automobiles. Running up to the mid-term elections of 2010, Jenny Beth and Mark shot a video of the two of them jet-setting around America in a private plane. In the Tea Party world, this YouTube video was met with mixed reactions. Most of the smaller groups that had, in essence, been franchised at the local level, were angry for the lack of support from the national Patriots organization. Here you had Meckler and Martin flying in style to speak at small rallies while the local organizers wondered how to pay the tab, which included the cost of porta potty rentals, signs, staging, and a multitude of other expenses. Putting on these events can easily run into the hundreds of thousands of dollars.

One known fact about the Tea Party Patriots is that it is not a Limited Liability Corporation. The organization was a 501C-3 when it was formed. This meant that the organization could not endorse candidates. A C-3 is supposed to be a teaching organization. Jenny Beth and company got around this little snafu by holding rallies and speaking about the Constitution. Thus, they were able to keep enjoying the benefits of millions of dollars in donations without paying taxes on any of the proceeds.

What began as Tax Day rallies over government spending and waste quickly spread across the fruited plain. Groups formed in Dallas, Texas, San Antonio, Denver, Sacramento and Lexington, Kentucky. In fact, they sprouted up so quickly that the Internal Revenue Service could not keep up with C-3 applications. In the Dallas-Fort Worth metropolitan area alone there are at least a half-dozen groups comprised of hundreds of thousands of regular participants. One of them, headed by Katrina Pierson of Dallas, boasts in excess of 100,000 members and is still growing.

The interesting part of the remarkable success of these nationwide organizations, however, was that the mainstream media (NBC, CBS, ABC, CNN, etc.) refused to cover the story. They all featured little snippets about the Tea Party on the evening news, but other than that, they didn't give it much attention. On the other hand, talk show giants and conservative leaders covered the story with gusto. Radio legend Rush Limbaugh talked about it on his show for quite some time. Keep in mind, Limbaugh's regular audience numbered in the tens of millions weekly, so it's easy to understand how rapidly the news about the nationwide Tea Party groups would have spread. Truth be known, I have often wondered, *how do you ignore a story in Hartford of 10,000-plus screaming and unhappy folks dressed like Patrick Henry and standing on the state house steps?*

But they did.

This was the actual beginning or the first indication to the general public that the media had no interest in being supportive of anything conservative. It was the first glimpse into just how biased and deep in the tank they were for Barack Obama. The legacy media's obvious bias was to become major fuel for the fledgling movement as well.

To add even more energy to the Tea Party movement (*as if it did not already have enough*), in June of 2009, Obama bowed to the King of Saudi Arabia and delivered (in the Tea Party's eyes) a passionate, sympathetic speech toward Muslims in Cairo, Egypt. Obama's anti-American speech in Egypt poured gasoline on a bonfire of seething emotion. The President's conciliatory words and the photo of him bowing to a Muslim King inspired radio talents like Alex Jones, Rush Limbaugh, Sean Hannity, Mark Levin and countless other to spring into action. Consequently, the pictures spread like wildfire on Facebook, Twitter and the internet. For Alex Jones, who was already convinced that Obama was a Muslim plant in the White House, this latest development only served to send him into orbit. While Limbaugh is a professed conservative, by comparison, Jones is a Limbaugh on steroids, whom some in the Tea Party movement view as a fringe figure, due to his stance that 9/11 was an "inside job."

I mention Alex Jones because he has a rather widespread audience on the radio and the internet. But more importantly because he wields much influence in terms of the Tea Party movement. By the summer of 2009, the Tea Party was being transformed from just Tax Day frustrations into a total *hyper-conservative* movement (my own term). Allow me to explain because this becomes increasingly relevant as we close in on the 2012 Presidential Election.

While the left, or if you will, the Democrats, like to accuse Rush of being a right wing fringe wacko, he is rather tame in comparison to folks like Alex Jones. For instance, Rush will report the blowing up of the Federal Building in Oklahoma City as a terrible tragedy. Alex Jones would not only report the incident, but posit his theory about why he believes our federal government was behind it, naming names and offering motives. For Patriots who love a good conspiracy theory, Jones gives them plenty of fodder for many beer drinking sessions around the old campfire. He is one of the chief architects behind the notion of President George W. Bush and the New World Order (Jones accuses the Bush family of being NWO members) as responsible parties for the attacks of September 11, 2001. Keep this in mind because it comes back into play later in the book. Suffice it to say, Jones brought an element of *"Hate thy Government"* into the Tea Party movement, not to mention a significant amount of paranoia surrounding the evilness of America's government.

When one wants to truly analyze the Tea Party movement and its origins, one must think about *"who"* comprises the membership of the movement to get a grasp on its meteoric rise in popularity.

I have been asked many times over the last several years, *who makes up the base of the Tea Party?* My stock answer is this: The Tea Party is comprised of the old Christian Coalition, Reagan Democrats, hacked off conservative Republicans, and conspiracy theorists. Back in 1989, Presidential candidate Reverend Pat Robertson had taken his religious programming to the streets and formed what was known as the Christian Coalition. Membership, of course, is in dispute, but everyone agrees that membership numbered in the millions. The strongest base came from the old South. States like Tennessee, North Carolina, Virginia, and Alabama held the strongest contingents for the movement. It is no secret that these states are also some of the strongest areas for card-carrying members (metaphor) who love to wave the Gadsden flag as well.

Political history tells us that for well over 100 years, Texas was largely a Democrat Garden of Eden. The Lone Star State was home to some of the greatest Democrat leaders in American history. By today's standards, these same Dems, like former Democrat Congressman Phil Graham turned Republican Senator Phil Graham have jumped off the Democrat bandwagon and joined the right side of the aisle. The former Senator was pretty much forced into doing so because of his constituency down in Bryan, Texas, which forced him to the right. The states listed above and many more are also known as the Bible Belt, for good reason. The Baptist, Methodist, Church of Christ, and Pentecostal churches, among others, are extremely influential in the Deep South. When the Democrat Party began drifting to the left in mid-80's, Graham's base in College Station, Texas demanded that he pull up his blue dog stake and transfer it to the elephant pen.

The mass media likes to label the Tea Party as racist, demagogues, right wing fanatics, and a litany of other derogatory terminology, but the truth of the matter is the majority of the Tea Party memberships across America are simply average Americans who love God, their country, their families, and neighbors. They own small businesses or work in middle-class occupations, attend PTA meetings, coach little league baseball, and go bowling on Wednesday nights. They are not wealthy for the most part, but in turn, they don't hate the wealthy because they are rich. They love liberty, freedom, and the right to succeed or fail on one's own merits. One must also understand that the average Tea Party member also attends church regularly and believes that basic human rights stem from the Bible, the Constitution, and Bill of Rights. This is a very key factor into discerning why and explaining the rapid expansion and growth of the Tea Party.

Most of the Tea Party Nation and its members began researching America's origins almost immediately and in a very serious way. They began buying books written by Glenn Beck and books entitled, *The 5,000 Year Leap*. They began holding weekly or monthly meetings in people's homes, then expanding to local churches. Tea Party leaders passed out copies of Ayn Rand's novel, *Atlas Shrugged*, about a character named John Galt and the quest for individual liberty. *The Roots of Obama's Rage* by Dinesh D'Souza immediately became a best seller upon its release.

Why? Why this starvation for political and patriotic knowledge? Why were books and videos being sold by the million, even some published as far back as 1957?

There is little doubt that the bulk of these sales came from Tea Party homes. In a simple sentence, *the conservative world known as the Tea Party could sense that something was going on in America and it was not for the better!*

For the first time in their collective lives, they were witnessing something they viewed as sinister happening in their government. These religiously and politically conservative voters could not understand why a President would bow to a King. They could not understand why he was attacking big business and Wall Street, all the while stripping taxpayers' dollars to bail these very industries out. Reports were beginning to surface on how he granted green energy companies hundreds of millions of their dollars, only to find out that the owners of these companies were, in fact, the Presidents own campaign fundraising bundlers. They could see the depths of corruption consuming their White House and the word was spreading fast across America's conservative voting base.

The stories coming from people's radios by Alex Jones, Rush Limbaugh, Sean Hannity and Glenn Beck were serving to fuel this anger even further. There were payoffs to the green energy companies, guns being sold to drug lords in Mexico, and, of course, Jones infusing his tin foil hat conspiracy theories like the government taking over America and imprisoning anyone who disagreed into FEMA camps. The FEMA camp for government dissidents was, of course, another piece to the puzzle that held the Patriots attention. Between the radio hosts explaining how Obama was attacking their religious faith, the taxing of wealth, job losses due to Obama, the

Wall Street payoffs, the shoving of green energy (which doesn't work) down our collective throats, rising gasoline prices (because of Obama) and so many more juicy topics, we were now ready for an explosion of patriotism.

The summer of '09 brought us a barrage of Tea Party expansion, plus a new twist. Glenn Beck began the organizing of his now famous 9-12 rally in Washington, D.C. Beck started a movement of 9 Principles and 12 Values that he hoped would "Re-Found" America with 56 *Re-Founders* from our House and Senate elected officials. Beck's goal was to hold a massive rally, then implement a few days later his *Re-Founders* to restore America. To do this, he decided to hold a major rally with these core principles involved. The 9 principles are:

1. America is good.

2. I believe in God and He is the center of my life.

3. I must always try to be a more honest person than I was yesterday.

4. The family is sacred. My spouse and I are the ultimate authority, not the government.

5. If you break the law, you pay the penalty. Justice is blind and no one is above it.

6. I have a right to life, liberty and the pursuit of happiness, but there is no guarantee of equal results.

7. I work hard for what I have and I will share it with who I want to. The government cannot force me to be charitable.

8. It is not un-American for me to disagree with authority or to share my personal opinion.

9. The government works for me. I do not answer to them, they answer to me.

After the 9 principles Beck submitted for America's approval came the 12 Values:

1. Honesty
2. Reverence
3. Hope
4. Thrift
5. Humility
6. Charity
7. Sincerity
8. Moderation
9. Hard work
10. Courage
11. Personal responsibility
12. Gratitude/Friendship

These are the principles and values with which Beck was gathering steam to head to   Capitol Hill with an army of supporters. It is by no coincidence that he chose a date that holds particular sentimental value in America. Saturday, September 12, 2009, gave Glenn Beck the perfect day: he had a television and radio audience numbering in the millions; he had millions of disgruntled American patriots and worried Christians who agreed with him; he had a plan; he had the venue; and he had the assistance to pull it off. The stage was now set for an event of epic proportions.

TWO

AMERICAN VALUES: TIME TO GET THE WORD OUT?

The success of the Tax Day rallies spawned by Rick Santelli can be explained fairly easily. The American people had a pent up anger from the exorbitant spending by both George Bush and Barack Obama. In unison, they wanted to vent, and in unison, they spoke their frustrations. They came out in the sun in the South and they came out in some cases to ice on the ground to speak in the North. They spoke and they spoke loudly. Nobody at the time realized it, but in one short day (which had been motivated by one short speech by one man in Chicago), an entire American political movement had begun.

This political movement now known as the Tea Party was being largely overlooked by the power brokers from either party in Washington. Michael Steele from the GOP in the early days of the movement did not give it much credibility or staying power. The power brokers of the Republican Party such as the Political Operatives of Karl Rove, Steele and the rest of the elitist in the GOP ivory tower thought, this will go away. In the beginning, it was clearly evident that none of the hierarchy was very concerned. The Tea Party faithful, dressed in their Revolutionary War regalia did not seem to be much of a threat to the Armani dressed suits inside in the Beltway. This would soon be changing.

What the Armani-clad operatives didn't know was that millions of phone calls were being made. Millions upon millions of emails were being sent. Millions upon millions of dollars were being raised and Tea Party organizations were springing up faster than weeds growing in the spring in Texas. New political power brokers were being ordained at the national level. Names like Governor Sarah Palin, Christine O'Donnell, Scott Brown, Jenny Beth Martin, Judson Phillips and Sharon Angle were becoming household known.

All the while these new political superstars were spreading the words of conservatism; the Tea Party was transforming itself from Tax Day overspending protest to a more constitutional restoration movement.

It wasn't to be long before these new voices of the grassroots would be regulars on news talk programs such as the Bill O'Reilly and the Sean Hannity shows on Fox News. The Tea Party was rapidly becoming the voice of the frustrated. The American people who had long held frustration dating back to Clinton and beyond now had a voice and an outlet to vent.

Names such as Kevin Jackson, Mark Levin, Michael Savage and more were becoming popular along with the Limbaugh's and Hannity's. All of these voices were now picking up on a common theme that was coursing through America's veins. Glenn Beck has been voicing it for some time, but now the "it" was spreading like wildfire. The "IT" that was spreading was the anger and the fear that our government was out of control and that the government was actually undermining traditional America with a liberal and socialist viewpoint.

There is little question that this had taken some time to resonate in the nation. Conservative America had taken a beating going back to the early 1970's and they had "had enough!" You were now seeing a dramatic rise in homeschooling. Lindsey M. Burke, a Research Assistant in the Domestic Policy Studies Department at the Heritage Foundation, completed a study on homeschooling in 2009. Homeschooling of America's children had risen by some 74% between 1999 and 2009. The reason why? Much of the rise was a direct result of the liberal policies of not allowing God to be mentioned in the classroom anymore. The fact is also that the homeschoolers felt like the government had way too much involvement in their children's education and indoctrination was a major concern.

America was now on the cusp of beginning a revival of traditional American values.

With the beginning of the snatching back of her children from the clutches of an abusive government, conservative America was also immersing itself in learning all it could about our Founding Fathers. Not only was the Tea Party faithful siphoning all the knowledge it could about our founder's true intentions and beliefs, they were also out on the streets teaching this knowledge. Every rally from the summer of 2009 and on had Benjamin Franklin and Paul Revere teaching constitutional information. Booths were set up at most rallies where the local sponsoring Tea Party would hand out pocket Constitutions for small donations.

Little doubt exists in the mind of Tea Party conservatives that America is in a moral and ethical tailspin of sorts. One must understand the origins of when most of the tailspin began. Keep in mind that most of the Tea Party following are conservative Americans with very deep Christian and Biblical values. While there is a percentage that is, in fact, Jewish and Atheist, the fact is that the vast majority are from the Christian side of the aisle.

According to a Houston Chronicle poll and article in 2012, some 90% of all Americans claim to believe in God. While some 90% of Americans claim to acknowledge God at some level, some 80% claim to be practicing Christians of one faith or another.

With these numbers in mind, this would explain the outrage that the Tea Party has embraced regarding the removal of God from everything we hold dear. God is vitally important in government for the average Tea Party member. Tea Party supporters believe, rightfully so, that God was very instrumental in setting up America in the first place.

Not to get too far off track here, but if you look at our judicial system, most of our laws involving man against man laws are based on Biblical principles. Thou shalt not steal, thou shall not commit murder, thou shalt not covet, etc., etc. The Tea Party believes that all morality stems from the Holy Bible or the Jewish Torah.

In fact, most of our governmental systems were even set up on a loosely based Roman Empire representative system. The Roman Empire had Senators, Representatives, and Governors. In fact, the very person that ordered the crucifixion of Jesus Christ was Governor Pontius Pilot. This system of government stood for many centuries.

The point of this pseudo-history trek was to briefly explain most of the Christian base that comprises the Tea Party recognizes that our nation and governmental origins stem from biblical principles.

President George Washington stated: "While we are zealously performing the duties of good citizens and soldiers, we certainly ought not to be inattentive to the higher duties of religion. To the distinguished character of Patriot, it should be our highest glory to add the more distinguished character of Christian."[1]

President John Adams stated: "Suppose a nation in some distant Region should take the Bible for their only law Book, and every member should regulate his conduct by the precepts there exhibited! Every member would be obliged in conscience, to temperance, frugality, and industry; to justice, kindness, and charity towards his fellow men; and to piety, love, and reverence toward Almighty

---

1   *The Writings of Washington, pp. 342-343.*

God ... What a Utopia, what a Paradise would this region be."[2] I could literally fill a book with nothing but quotes from our Founding Fathers regarding the importance of Biblical principles in governing America.

When wondering "why" the Tea Party is so very patriotic and passionate about America, this is it. America's Tea Party is fueled by a passion for our nation that stems from its very heart and core belief system. The average Patriot knows in their heart that from our Pilgrims on the Mayflower to our Founding Fathers of James Madison, Thomas Jefferson, John Adams and the rest, God played a very vital role in how our nation was to be set up and operated. Our rights and freedoms stem from human rights granted to us by our very Lord and God, not from government. And this is what is fueling this passion that is sweeping across America.

When Barack Obama was elected on the mantra of "We will fundamentally transform America," shivers ran down the spine of those who would become your average Tea Party member. These were not the sorts of terminology or quotes that presidential candidates had used in the past. "Yes, your energy prices will necessarily skyrocket under my administration," to quote from a Barack Obama campaign address in San Francisco, California. Conservative America was shuddering on election night of 2008 and for good reason.

While the organization had not yet been implemented, millions of these Christian socially and fiscally conservative Americans were already in panic mode. They knew something was wrong. Sean Hannity had just spent months playing the now infamous video clips of the Reverend Jeremiah Wright spewing "your chickens have come home to roost" and the rest of his hate-filled sermons from his Chicago Church. Hannity, Limbaugh, and the rest were speaking daily of Obama's actual birth location and this had the Patriots in a frenzy as well.

---

2   *Diary and Autobiography of John Adams, Vol. III, p. 9.*

Between the birth location, the hate-spewing rhetoric from a supposed Christian Minister, the questionable energy ideology, the fundamental changing of America, along with the Hope and Change mantra, America was now set for a huge backlash. Keep in mind that this backlash is not some small irreverent band of people with a bad attitude. This is potentially 40 plus million irate Americans with a bad attitude toward people that are intentionally trying to harm the United States.

This reminds me of when Mohandas Gandhi went to visit the British Royalty in his palace. He is sitting in the Viceroy's office and the British Monarch said, "So, Mr. Gandhi, just how do plan on overthrowing the British Empire? You have no guns or army and we are the mightiest military on earth. Gandhi responded very softly and politely, Your Highness, what do you plan on doing with 500 million people that do not desire to cooperate any longer?"

I do not know if Gandhi actually articulated that line in real life, but it appears in the movie Gandhi, which won many Academy Awards and starred the award-winning actor Ben Kingsley. I always thought of that line in reference to this Tea Party movement. Just what does our government plan on doing with 40 million people that are both armed and tired of cooperating with tyranny?

While the internet was in play during the George W. Bush election cycles, it wasn't nearly as important as it was during the elections of Barack Obama. By the 2012 election cycle, the internet lived in most American homes and it seemed as though everyone under the age of 40 owned a smart phone or iPad. Wi-Fi had sprung up in every McDonalds and Starbucks in America and every potential voter was merely a click away. And make no mistake about it, the Obama camp knew how to capitalize on this technology.

Notice I said a moment ago, under the age of 40? This is instrumental because the average age of a conservative voter is over 40. Due to the fact that many, if not most of your 25-year-olds, do own the smartphones or iPad's and most of your 50 plus-year-olds do not, now you can readily see the problem with information. The Republican Party was simply not able to utilize the information highway to the degree that the Democrats had seized upon.

Facebook became a massive marketing tool for the Democrats as well. Going into the 2012 elections, it had over 1 billion regular users, and the Dems knew how to use social media to its advantage. This became a huge handicap for the Republican Party.

The anger in the Tea Party was not just smoldering, it was boiling! The Tea Party was all over Facebook and Twitter. They were getting the word out about Obama's crimes against America. They had spread the word about what they believed was actually Obama's crimes against freedom and liberty. They were actually doing a grand job of rousing anger against the administration. They were very prepared to hit the streets and get a good conservative elected. The only problem was the Republicans had decided in the smoke-filled backrooms of Washington to nominate a moderate in Governor Mitt Romney.

While the Tea Party messaging of patriotism, honor, valor, fiscal conservatism (lower taxes and less government waste and spending), pro-life, ridding America of Obama-Care, a strong military, balancing the budget and so much more was resonating, the elephants had put up a moderate. The Tea Party wanted a candidate that would tell America what Obama really was. They wanted a candidate with Ronald Reagan's articulation ability and John Wayne's patriotism. They wanted a candidate that would stand tall like Clint Eastwood and tell Barack Obama to hit the road, Jack.

By the summer of 2012, the Tea Party was not only in disarray, it was also severely depressed. They could not understand why the GOP establishment was ignoring it. And thus, the hatred of Karl Rove (Republican Operative) was growing daily. They (the Patriots) felt shunned and ostracized.

Meanwhile out in Iowa, you had a conservative radio talk show host by the name of Steve Deace. Steve's daily radio show is based on Christianity and politics; somehow he has managed to infuse the two together. His show began to expand its listener base – particularly in the conservative trenches. In conservative circles in the Midwest, Steve is one of those folks who's either loved or hated; there doesn't seem to be a middle ground for his popularity.

Steve had begun his rant against Romney, spending a couple of hours a day railing against the Massachusetts Governor. He was pounding Romney on the fact that he is a Latter Day Saint in lieu of say, a Baptist or a Methodist. He was berating him for instituting Romney Care (The Massachusetts Health Care Plan) and the fact that the law had a $50 abortion co-pay provision. He was not so much after him for being wealthy, but for the fact that Romney's Bain Capital had supported or funded certain companies. Deace even went so far as to say that Romney was a member of a cult.

I do want to clarify one point here: I am not berating Deace in particular. The fact is, there were many Steve Deace's across America, but he is one with whom I am familiar on a personal level.

Steve was spending all his airtime on a personal mission to make sure that Romney was not elected President.

I, on the other hand, knew we had two choices. For me, that was the reality of the situation. It did not make any difference to me that the Republicans might have been wrong, as it did to Steve. It is what it is. Romney was the nominee. That was the end of the conversation to me on a personal level. I could not undo what had been done. On an even more personal level, I knew that out of the crop of 2012 candidates, Mitt Romney was the only one that had a chance of defeating Obama. I will expound on that later. Deace now had his mission for the next three- to-four months; he had Romney in his crosshairs.

For me, this was becoming a personal mission as well. I wanted to convince Steve Deace that he was no different from Barack Obama

– a demagogue with a microphone! Steve would ridicule Romney for being a "non-Christian," or rather, not someone with your typical mainstream Christian beliefs, yet he supported Newt Gingrich. Keep in mind that Governor Romney had been married to the same woman for some 40 years, raised a herd of children, and had 20-plus grandchildren. Gingrich, on the other hand, had a less than stellar record in the marriage department. Can we say "hypocrite" for Deace?

One of Deace's principle targets was Romney's health-care bill in his state. My argument was fairly simple in nature. Yes, Romney had signed a health-care bill that Obama was using to protect against the attacks on his Obamacare. Here was my stand on the matter:

Romney was the Governor of a small Northeast state. His elected representatives had come to him with an idea for a statewide health-care plan for its citizens. Romney said fine, if this is what the citizens want and we can afford it, then we will do it. All the players got involved and they came up with something that made everyone happy. Romney signed it. My argument was, "This is what Governors do!" Governors do things in their states because they can and that is their job. It is not like he is forcing it down everyone's throat and destroying our national healthcare system like Obama.

Needless to say, the only retort Deace had for me was, "I have to vote my moral convictions." I can tell you this much, in the end, the vote in Iowa was in fact, close. I attribute Romney losing in Iowa and the state going blue to Steve Deace and his clones that follow him with as much fervor as Ron Paul's or Reverend Jim Jones's supporters. They drink the Deace Kool-Aid and they kneel and bow and praise at the altar of Deace. They were wrong! Steve voted ideology over political reality. He cast his vote for either Ron Paul or Newt. He wrote in his vote and thus wasted it. It essentially became a vote for Obama. The exact things he railed against: Obamacare, national security, abortion and all the rest, he, in fact, voted for by supporting Barack Obama. Newt was not going to win, Paul could not win, but Romney could have as he was the nominee.

The Tea Party committed suicide in 2012. They performed heroically by getting the word about conservatism out to the public. They did marvelously at explaining how evil Obama was for America. They campaigned for conservatives across America and they worked tirelessly for the cause.

But.

They could not and would not agree on whom to support for President. Their very fiber or DNA, if you will, is what prevented them from even attempting to become victorious. The Tea Party is so entrenched in supporting the grassroots that it cannot bring itself to unify behind one candidate.

When you have some 25 million registered Tea Party faithful and another 40 million who think and vote like the registered members, this is a massive voting bloc. If even 20% change their minds or decide to leave the ranch, you can literally sway a Presidential election with that amount of votes. And that is exactly what happened.

Of course, the Ron Paul devotees will deny it, but it happened. Yes, there was a bit of voter fraud in Ohio and several other isolated spots, but not 12 or 20 or 30 million vote's worth. Had those Tea Party, Ron Paul and moral-conviction voters shown up and voted with some "political practicality and rational thought," we would not have Barack Obama destroying America today.

My argument was and still is that Governor Mitt Romney might not have passed the Steve Deace Christian qualification test, but so what? He was certainly a good father and husband. He loved America and he was a great businessman. He knew how to create a roaring economy and he did not lie to the American people. I have had friends who are LDS tell me the Mormons believe that Jesus will come back and set up his Kingdom in Salt Lake City, Utah. My stance was simple: if that's the case, then who better to be President than a Mormon? That Mormon President is going to do everything in his power to protect Salt Lake. Because Salt Lake sits in the confines of the continental United States, I will have to feel pretty safe. This made perfect sense to me.

Allow me to throw this hypothetical theory out there. What would have happened if the Tea Party had united behind Senator Rick Santorum? I am staying on Iowa for the simple reason that it is the first state in the nation to give a candidate a head of steam. Iowa is the start of the serious process of accumulating the mass amounts of money they need to operate a successful campaign. Santorum would have left Iowa with a clear victory in the media, thus enabling him to raise copious amounts of money over the next week leading into New Hampshire.

Santorum is from Pennsylvania. While not a bordering state, it is not that far from New Hampshire. The Granite State has a fairly active Tea Party community. Therefore, Santorum could have had a decent showing in New Hampshire and probably came in second behind Romney. This would have sent him to South Carolina where the Tea Party is enormously powerful and would no doubt have won The Palmetto State.

The point I am making is that given the lack of cohesiveness of the Tea Parties in Iowa and around America, the conservative base lost large. Why? Why are the Tea Parties unwilling to work together and speak with one voice? Why is it so hard for the Des Moines Tea Party to work with the Dubuque Tea Party? Simply put, the Dubuque Tea Party will only support Ron Paul. Thus, persuading them to support another candidate who is actually more viable is out of the question. Congressman Ron Paul is pitching a philosophy of Libertarianism and the world knows it. The world knows that in order to win the White House, you must pick up several of the deep Southern states like Florida, Texas, and Tennessee. With Paul's record on legalizing prostitution, drugs, and his performances in the debates in which he expressed his willingness to allow Iran to garner nuclear weapons, his ideology doesn't fly in Knoxville, Tennessee. Again, why are we wasting time on ideology when it is simply not electable? Santorum was, at least, viable and with enough pressure from the Tea Party, he could have been sold to the Republican establishment.

From early 2009 through 2010 and the incredible victories the Tea Parties had amassed across America, in a remarkably short period of time, the message was resonating in America: The Tea Party was a force to be reckoned with! The midterm victories of 2010 was not a fluke or accident. When you have a swing of that many House seats, something is most definitely going on. The message of lower taxes, smaller government, less government intrusion, and fiscal sanity was hitting home runs across America. The message of ridding America of Obamacare was also hitting a grand slam at every town hall and campaign stop.

So what happened in 2011? Why did the Tea Party all but evaporate? Why wasn't the Tea Party screaming in unison behind one candidate? We know about Dubuque, Iowa, but what about the rest of Iowa and America?

I believe the lackluster performance of the Tea Party in the campaigning season of 2011 for the 2012 Presidential elections can be traced to two events and the internet. While the internet was one of the reasons for the Tea Party's meteoric rise to prominence, I believe it is also one of the reasons it harmed itself. Combine the internet with a couple of events of such massive proportions, I also believe that the average Tea Party individual sat back and said: "How do we top this?"

THREE

NO, HONESTLY, I AM NOT A WITCH?

By the 2010 midterm elections, it was now clearly evident that the *'ragtag band of misfits'* (as the Democrats and Republican hierarchy liked to refer to them) were now beginning to cause much more mischief than just protesting. These *'misfits'* had decided to begin changing Washington, D.C. and they were not subtle about it.

The first indications that the Tea Party was a growing threat came when the speeches at their events began to change. When the first protest began back in late early 2009, the speeches were comprised mostly of *"too much government,"* *"we are being taxed too heavily,"* and we *"need to cut government waste and spending."*

When President Barack Obama's speeches began taking the tone of *'we have too many guns and there is too much gun violence'* in our land, the 2nd Amendment groups across America found an ally in the Tea Party. We began seeing representatives from the NRA and other major gun groups joining the Patriot chorus at events. Then came the "Pro-Life" coalitions. Due to the Tea Party's theme of patriotism, life, liberty, human rights, God and a mostly Christian-based lining to everything they stood for, now the anti-abortion coalitions found a much larger platform to campaign from with the Tea Party.

Almost simultaneously, you had 'homeschooling coalitions' joining and setting up booths at events alongside 'anti-Common Core education' organizations. Toss in radio mega-star Glenn Beck's '9-12' groups and you now had a political force to be reckoned with. The common theme amongst all of the Tea Party groups was fairly simple. We want conservatism to flourish in all forms and we want the radical liberalism to stop and stop now. Cries and chants of *"we don't want your Hope and Change"* (referring to Barack Obama's 2008 campaign theme) could be heard all across the fruited plain at every event.

As the summer of 2010 rolled around, Tea Party groups had mushroomed to well over 600 organized coalitions. Membership estimates in these groups ranged wildly from a few million to upwards of 40 million. The largest of these groups were Tea Party Patriots, Tea Party Nation, Tea Party.net and Tea Party Express. Those four groups alone accounted for literally millions of members and when you combine the large groups of Orlando, San Antonio, Garland, Texas (150,000 est.), Phoenix (tens of thousands) to name but a few, you can readily ascertain the national membership count might very well be 30-40 million.

With these sorts of numbers in play, the Tea Party began searching for candidates to begin replacing the dreaded RINO's (the old moniker, Republican In Name Only, as the Tea Party began referring to the more moderate Republicans).

The Patriots found their first national superstar candidate in the state of Delaware. Christine O'Donnell had been a political operative for many years with the Republican establishment at one level or another. Her political career has mostly revolved around various advocacy issues which involved Christian-based principles. While in college, she became involved in the George H. W. Bush and Dan Quayle campaign for the College Republicans. She had also attended the 1992 and 1996 Republican National Convention where she was a commentator for CNN and other networks giving the "young person's" viewpoint on convention issues and happenings.

Afterward, she spent the next decade or so being an advocate for many organizations and issues. None of this experience would properly prepare her for what was to come when she entered the race (midterm 2010) for Joe Biden's vacated United States Senate seat in Delaware when he became Vice President.

Because of O'Donnell's hyper-conservatism, she instantly became a Tea Party rock star princess. Christine O'Donnell rode the wave of anti-establishment, anti-big government, lower taxes and mass Tea Party support to a victory in the Republican primary against the much hated (RINO) former Congressman and Delaware Governor Mike Castle.

Between the support of the Tea Party's reigning queen Sarah Palin and the volunteer base she amassed (because of the Tea Party), this relative political unknown shocked the political world by defeating an entrenched political Godzilla (in Delaware). If I live to be one hundred, I will never forget the expression on GOP operative Karl Rove's face during his interview on Fox News when this political neophyte young lady was announced to have defeated the Republican establishment's choice, Mike Castle. It was a look of total astonishment.

As someone famous once said, "*all good things must come to an end*" and end they did for Christine. O'Donnell by winning had managed to alienate most if not all of the Republican Party leadership. Rove offered nearly zero support for her and to this day it is widely rumored that it was Rove himself that led a black-ops campaign behind the scenes to ensure that O'Donnell did not win the general election against the Democrat challenger.

Almost immediately after the improbable win over Castle, O'Donnell began having to feign questions about her personal finances. Then came charges from one of her former campaign managers, Kristin Murray, about O'Donnell's "fake" conservatism. This was done in her run-up to the general election when Murray sent out recorded "robo-calls" charging O'Donnell with a laundry list of grievances, including her paying her rent with campaign money.

By the fall of 2010, the shine had most certainly worn off of Christine O'Donnell's halo as a Tea Party princess. Her campaign was in shreds and it would not be until many months later we would all find out that it was a coup d'état led by non-other than O'Donnell's former rival Mike Castle. The body punches of O'Donnell's character came fast and furiously to the political novice. She absorbed charges of not paying her campaign staffers, wasting money, and misappropriating funds. She even absorbed character assassination charges of having been a *witch* in her younger days.

The fatal blow for her campaign came from Christine O'Donnell's own lips in a late-campaign television advertisement. Any political operative will tell you that if an opponent makes an outlandish charge, simply ignore it. People will often think it's a desperate move on the part of the person casting the aspersion in the first place. But alas, remember, we are dealing with a Tea Party political novice here.

This was one of the major problems with Tea Party devotee's getting involved in high-level politics. Had Christine "earned her chops" by running for a State Senate seat, I am pretty sure it would have been much different for her. Had she run for anything beneath a United States Senate seat, she would have been better off.

The winter of 2011 after a debacle in Indianola, Iowa (details later in this book), Christine came to visit me in Des Moines. She had called me and asked if I could set up a meet and greet for her so she could do a press conference and sell her new book. She came to town and a small gathering of fans greeted her warmly. She gave a short speech and signed some books. Afterward, we (her father, former campaign manager Matt Moran, and I) went to dinner.

I knew I should probably not have asked the question, but I

simply could not restrain myself. "So Christine, tell me, who was the idiot that thought running the witch commercial was a good idea?" I asked.

Many things can be said of Christine O'Donnell, but the one truth I know personally is that she is a lady, and a totally gracious person. After my rather asinine question, she simply smiled, chuckled and said, "Many were responsible," and went on with the conversation. Of course, everyone in the Tea Party world knew it was a concoction of Matt Moran and Christine O'Donnell.

In essence, for those who don't remember, O'Donnell had been charged with having been a witch. This was particularly negative for her because she had spent so many years campaigning on Christian values. The advocacies included, "don't masturbate, it is adultery," "don't have premarital sex," and the list went on. When the "bombshell" hit that she had been a witch in her younger days, of course, this was a major story and became national headlines in the political sphere.

This is when in desperation to clear her name, O'Donnell hit the airwaves with the now famous, *I am not a Witch* television ad. Yes, she actually purchased time and taped a commercial to tell the world she was *NOT* a witch. It was this advertisement that did not just become a bombshell, it became a thermonuclear warhead that eviscerated her campaign.

Christine O'Donnell would not be alone in being a campaigning novice who self-destructed. There would be many more in the coming days and years. Probably the most notable would be this statement: "You won't get pregnant if you're raped."

Those utterly astonishing words were said by none other than United States Congressman Todd Akin of Missouri. Akin became an instant Tea Party favorite with his opposition to "No Child Left Behind" which he fought against because he believes that education should be left up to the states. His stance on pro-life, guns, and the

Constitution made him an instant hit with his Missouri Patriots, who are incredibly large in number.

It is this grassroots support from the Tea Party which led the Congressman to a victory over the crowded field of Republican contenders. It is also the brash and brazen Tea Partyesque campaign style that buried the Congressman's campaign when it came to the general election against Democrat Claire McCaskill.

If one wants to throw away a perfectly successful United States Senate campaign, simply stand up and say, "Hey lady, don't worry about it, you won't get pregnant if you're raped and particularly if it is a legitimate rape." Of course, this was in response to questioning regarding his stand on Roe versus Wade and legalized abortion.

Akin, however, is somewhat of a victim in all of this. No, I am not defending the absolutely idiotic statement regarding rape. What is happening within these candidates' campaigns is that they begin reaching out to the Tea Party, not being aware that they're actually walking into a den of gnashing teeth embodied in a pack of political wolves.

Once they are welcomed by the Tea Party and garner the support of the Patriots, they are now required to keep "all" their principles or else they are excoriated and evicted by this prized voting bloc. Against all professional advice from experienced political operatives, the Tea Party will challenge quality candidates and force them to adhere to all of their politically far-right viewpoints.

In Akin's case, he is feebly trying to explain "why" he feels so strongly about abortion. He knows that if he qualifies his statement with "*I am opposed to abortion except in the cases of rape and incest,*" that this is not good enough for the pro-life factions of the Tea Party. Morally, yes, he should be totally opposed as a Christian, but politically treading into that very soft ground will cause you to end up in a bog and you will be mired down in quicksand, particularly with the Tea Party.

It is the campaigns of Todd Akin, Christine O'Donnell and many more that has caused the ostracization of the Tea Party from the mainstream Republican Party. These campaigns began much like a rocket. They accelerated quickly, did well for quite a while, then experienced major mechanical breakdowns (usually by the candidate themselves) and fizzled out in an embarrassing fashion.

Today, the Republican Party does everything it can to distance itself from the Tea Party. The Tea Party rejects the Republicans much like the black plague. The Patriots run around crossing their index fingers at Republicans all the while chanting "RINO-RINO" as if that candidate is evil. It is this political approach that gave us four more years of Barack Obama. Yes, my fellow Americans, you can thank the Tea Party for the re-election of Barack H. Obama as President of these United States.

FOUR

A GUY NAMED CRAIG AND HIS GROUPIES

Had you told me seven (7) years ago that I would have been involved with a cast straight out of a 1940's gangster movie (complete with James Cagney), I would have told you, you're nuts.

Have you ever known someone that the moment you meet them they just seem to be way too perfect? They always have the right answer, they always speak with authority and usually have enough intellect to make their argument seem to be very plausible. Meet Craig (I'm leaving his last name out of this for obvious reasons, but those who know me, know who I'm referencing here), everyone's favorite 'politics expert on everything.'

Remember Charlie? Charlie Gruschow is without question one of the nicest human beings you would ever meet. He is a cross between a fire-breathing dragon when it comes to anything dealing with our nation and the love thereof, and everyone's favorite teddy bear grandfather type. He is soft-spoken, incredibly polite and the moment you meet him, you instantly know he would give you the shirt off his back if need be.

The winter of 2011 (January or February), I was invited to a very nice townhouse complex in Des Moines, Iowa and told which meeting room to walk into. Charlie was hosting this particular gathering, which included many members of the Des Moines Tea Party.

The campaigning for the hearts and minds of Iowa Caucus goers was already in full swing. This is the time of the year when you can walk into a barber shop in a small town and meet a Governor visiting with farmers who are talking politics and fussing about grain prices all in the same conversation. This is the time in a presidential election cycle when you can stop by the John Deere dealership parts department and meet a Congressman or a Senator campaigning for President. I have to admit, it is unique and it is actually fun for a political junkie like myself.

It was at this particular meeting at Charlie's townhouse where I was handed brochures about the benefits of electing Herman Cain as the next President. It seemed that Charlie was planning a rally at the State Capitol in March to showcase Mr. Cain and his Tea Party friendly campaign rhetoric. This is also where I met Craig.

Going into this meeting, I honestly had zero intention of becoming as immersed into the local Iowa Tea Party scene as I was about to become. All I wanted to do was meet a few folks, with Charlie being my main target. It was my goal (and still is) to befriend every Tea Party group leader in America if at all possible. To date, I now know hundreds, but that was then, and this is now.

As I sat down while Charlie was laying out the agenda for the meeting, a warm smile in the next chair greeted me with a friendly handshake. His name was Craig. What I did not know at that time was, I had just met the spawn of Satan in the flesh.

As Charlie droned on about the impending Cain event, Craig would intermittently toss in something about his escapades on previous campaign incursions into Pennsylvania or this candidate or that candidate. Of course, to someone like me, who has volunteered in previous years for a candidate like Ronald Reagan but never knew him, this name-dropping was impressive. Craig seemed to know everyone on a personal level. My radar should have been activated, but at that time, I suppose it was on vacation because it definitely was not fine-tuned that day.

After Charlie had figured out 'who would sing the national anthem, which speakers would be in what order etc.,' it was decided to adjourn the meeting and I finally had a chance to visit with Mr. Gruschow himself. The longer I visited with Charlie, the more I decided that this was a guy with whom I would actually love to become friends. I did notice that Craig had also hung around after the meeting and politely inserted himself into Charlie's and my conversation. It was not rude or anything and he seemed to stay on topic (for the life of me today, I could not tell you what we talked about), but Craig did offer some what seemed like good advice for Charlie regarding the event.

I remember asking Charlie if there was anything I could help him with. He actually said 'yes' if I was willing. The event was to take place in a couple of weeks and would I mind dropping by a local Ford dealership to pick up a rental SUV? I was to drive it out to the corporate terminal at the Des Moines airport at 10:00 AM on Saturday and wait for Mr. Cain's private plane to arrive, then bring him back to the Capital.

This particular Saturday was not like most March days across America. The temperature was in the high 20's, little piles of snow were still visible in shaded areas, and the wind was blowing about 30 miles per hour. It wasn't just cold; it was damned cold.

My stomach was churning a little, my nerves were a bit shaky and I confess, I was a little star-struck by the opportunity to meet the hottest contestant in the quest for the nomination. At the time, Herman was either in first place or about to be; he was now a star who spent half his time on Fox News.

I pulled up to the awning in front of the corporate terminal, walked into the restroom to take care of some business, and nearly dropped my jaw. When I walked in, there was Mr. Cain standing at the sink washing his hands.

I looked up at him (as he is about 3 or 4 inches taller than myself) and said "Hello, Mr. Cain." He greeted me with a huge grin and a bellowing "Hello Ken and how are you today?"

As we walked out to the SUV, Herman did ask if it was a Ford. I, of course, had to ask him, "Why, will you only ride in a Ford Mr. Cain?" He promptly informed me that Ford was the only company that would not take taxpayers' money for a bailout, which was why they were the only car company he supported. He'd even sold his family's cars and bought new Fords. Wow, now this is a principled candidate! Of course, I don't know the validity of that statement, but it sounded great.

His videographer, a young cowboy whose hat happened to feature a documentary filmmaker from Hollywood, sat in the front seat. Herman sat in the back with my wife, who is from New Zealand, complete with the Kiwi accent. I relay this information because once he said hello and heard her accent, he kept telling us about his fondness for the tiny nation way *Down Under*. Add his love for her accent and her easygoing sense of humor and Mr. Cain had just made a new friend.

About three stoplights into our journey to the State Capital, I remember thinking, while listening to their conversation, *this guy is getting pretty personal with my wife*, but I let it slide until I reached the fourth light. That's when Cain finally piped up and asked the train-stopping question, "So Ken, tell me, what do you think I need to do to get elected President?"

The first thought that came to mind, the one I articulated was, "Isn't that a question you should ask your campaign manager Mark Block?"

"I want your opinion Mr. Crow."

"Are you sure you want my honest opinion?"

"Yep, give it to me and don't hold back!"

Alright, he asked. And he was about to get it with both barrels.

It had been two weeks since that meeting at Charlie's place and in that amount of time, I had received phone calls from some of Cain's volunteers in Iowa (whom I'd met at Charlie's). These phone calls, for the most part, were on the hysterical side, and asked for my opinion about this breach of trust, this rumor and that rumor, and many more distressing developments. One of the big rumors was that Cain – or rather, Mark Block, had hired an openly gay man to run some of his national campaign messaging. The person who called me was upset because Cain was campaigning on traditional family values, yet had brought in a homosexual fellow as a senior campaign official. She was concerned that if the media found out about it, it would hurt his electability.

I based my response to Herman on this information. "Mr. Cain, do you really want to be President of the United States?"

At first he laughed at me, then responded with a resounding, "Yes, of course he wanted to be President!"

Then I dropped the hammer on him.

"Mr. Cain, if you want to be President of these United States, you need to fire every one of your staff, spend $3 million dollars and hire Dick Morris, shut up, and let him run your campaign. You need a high-profile manager, whether it be Dick Morris or someone else, but that person needs to be a heavyweight. Then you need to do what they say to do. This will help with fundraising, seriousness, and credibility for your campaign."

Everybody in the SUV was stone-cold silent; in fact, you could hear everyone breathing.

His response told me everything I needed to know about his campaign. Isn't it strange how life works out? This man lied through his teeth in the first 10 minutes of me knowing him. He responded, "I don't have $3 million dollars and if I did, I would not spend it on a campaign manager."

That is when I countered with, "In the last two weeks you have raised several million dollars Mr. Cain, plus you could personally write a check to bring someone in at that level. I guess you don't really want to be President then do you."

He didn't speak to me again until the trip back to the airport. The tragedy in that conversation was that I was right; he could have become President had he had the right management team and been handled correctly. Many of the mistakes that besieged his campaign in the coming months would have been handled in the right fashion and he could have actually landed a top position (if not the nomination, certainly a VP slot), simply because of his enormous popularity and the fact he was Southern and an African- American. But alas, he did not listen to me. Then came the scandals with women, the Mark Block smoking video (this made national headlines, all of them negative), and many more amateurish mistakes that ended his campaign.

Shortly after the Cain event at the Capital (which was affectionately labeled as an ICE TEA rally) where everyone's toes became numb from the sub-freezing temperatures, I received a phone call from Craig. He called to invite me out for Chinese food.

The lunch confab was sort of a 'feeling out' meeting. We exchanged political ideologies, discussed what was wrong with the Tea Party, considered what we could do to cause an explosion of patriotism across our land, and strategized on how to take over the moderate Republican Party that can only seem to lose elections. All in all, it was a great meeting, where Craig and I saw eye-to-eye on many political topics, including, "We must consolidate these hundreds of Tea Party groups into one monster Tea Party!"

The reasoning back then, which is still relevant today, is that with no central leadership, the Tea Party is much like trying to herd cats. It needs to at least be unified in the sense that all Tea Party organizations are pointed in the same direction.

In the end, Craig had sold me with his political prowess (or at least I thought he had political prowess) and his extended reach with who he knew, what he knew, and for the length of time he had been in the political field as an operative.

The next day, I called Charlie and proposed a lunch meeting with Craig to discuss the possibility of holding a major rally event where tens of thousands of patriots would show up, have it nationally televised, and do it all under the banner of *Tea Party of America.* It was my idea to hold this event shortly after the Iowa Straw Poll and before the Iowa Caucuses, which were scheduled for the first days in January of 2012. Craig was now officially in the inner circle with trust and friendship.

What we were about to learn (unfortunately far too late) was that we had just invited the fox into the henhouse. If ever there was a truer form of a wolf in sheep's clothing, it would be Craig. He would come to epitomize the truest definition of everything the Tea Party stood against. He was a James Cagney in that he would (metaphorically) kill his own mother if it helped him further his prominence and political standing, and make him money.

Charlie and I were too naïve to be dealing with someone who was as politically ravenous as Jaws. We were trusting, we were (and still are) honest, and when we shook someone's hand, we believed that handshake meant something in terms of a promise or an agreement. We were raised to believe that a man stood by his handshake. Not Craig.

We were about to be embroiled with Satan in the flesh.

FIVE

THE BIRTH OF TEA PARTY OF AMERICA

After Charlie's and my lunch with Craig, I had decided we had hit on a brainstorm. We had all agreed that on a national scope, the only thing that would save America was a truly patriotic movement of epic proportions.

Back in 2011, America was still under the illusion that Barack Obama not only loved our nation but was actually trying to help her. We in the conservative movement knew better. This guy was piling on trillions of dollars of debt, gutting our military, seizing entire segments of our economic engine and destroying America's prestige globally. We knew it then, now the question was, how to get that message out to the masses?

Lest you think that Charlie and I had lost our minds, remember that both of us are devout Christians. This is relevant because we both have studied the Bible and know it fairly well. The Lord has several quotations in the New Testament that clearly state, *"you shall be known by the company you keep."* We had both come to the conclusion that when you look at Obama's White House, who his staff is, who his senior aides and top advisers are, it is easy to come to the conclusion that this man is not just devious, he is dangerous.

While we knew something was happening in the Middle East, we had no idea things could get as bad as they have. With the bulk of Obama's inner circle being Muslim (Valerie Jarett for one) and card-carrying members of the "Muslim Brotherhood," we knew this president was up to no good and the only way to do this was have an organization that became so powerful, we could actually sway the House of the Representatives and the Senate to impeach this president.

A wise person once said, "hindsight is 20/20" and in retrospect, while our ambitions were over-the-top in terms of desire, our predictions about Barack Obama have all come to pass. Since those initial lunch meetings, over a dozen nations in the Middle East and Northern Africa have fallen to Al-Qaeda, ISIS, Boko Haram and more. The nations that were having the "Arab Springs" are now under the control of the Muslim Brotherhood (except Egypt) or another terrorist organization. Millions have been tortured, millions have died and millions are still being rounded up and slaughtered, all while this president does nothing to stop the carnage. Any wonder why we were trying so desperately to organize and stop this president?

Now that you fully understand our motivation behind the movement (at least for Charlie and me), I can fully explain the "plan of action" to unify the movement and get all the members moving in the same direction.

Naively both Charlie and I thought that most, if not all, of the 600-plus organizations would be of the same mindset. That mindset being that we in the Tea Party shared similar goals and aspirations. Such goals and aspirations would, of course, be to construct a massive organization with all 20-million-plus members, all marching in lockstep to force Congress and the Senate into capitulating to whatever we wanted. Keep in mind that nothing we wanted was nefarious by nature; we only wanted our government to restore the liberties that have been stripped from us over the past decade or so. Of course, we wanted our nationally spending to be balanced, we wanted to put a stop to the piling up of debts we can never hope to pay back, and we wanted to cut some of the government institutions that are constitutionally illegal, such as the National Education Administration.

After several phone calls to attorneys with an explanation of what we wanted to do, we decided to incorporate as an IRS 501(C)3 and later form a Super-PAC where we could raise money, endorse, and support or attack candidates.

Tea Party of America was about to be legal. Then we could embark on our goal of unification to both save and restore our nation from the liberalism that was crippling our once prosperous land.

In retrospect, I can now see what Craig's entire motivation was, but at that time, we were so immersed in getting this organization up and running, neither Charlie or I could see what he was actually doing. Craig was constantly involved in the organization process. He assisted in selecting board members, shares to be distributed, and individuals who would hold specific positions. He had offered legal advice throughout the process, based upon "his previous experience" in which we had bought into and believed. Yes, all in all, Craig had made himself a valuable asset to what Charlie and I were trying to achieve.

To give you one example of how deep we allowed Craig to penetrate the process, Charlie and I had decided we needed a website. Neither of us knew anything about developing a website, other than we needed to own the domain name. I obtained the domain address and we began shopping web development companies to assist in the creation of our site. After obtaining development prices ranging from $10,000 up to $75,000, Craig informed us he had a "friend" who was a WordPress expert and would do it for a nominal fee of something like $2,500.

The part of this that was incredibly frustrating was that Charlie had a friend who had built us one for next to nothing, but Craig convinced us it was "out of touch, out of date and ugly." We decided to take a chance on Craig's advice and try the pretty, up-to-date version.

While we were still under the guise that Craig was a friend, what we did not know at the time was the web developer had left back doors open for himself and Craig to play in the backend of the website anytime they desired. Also, remember that Charlie and I were still under the naïve notion that just like us, Craig was doing all this for patriotic purposes. We had no idea at that time, but were about to find out the real motivation behind most of these Tea Party groups.

After the site was built and recruitment had begun, Charlie and I decided we needed to make a national splash, or a "coming out" party if you will. We both knew and discussed the only way to bring the other groups into the fold was to create something so large, it would force the membership to see the validity of unification, thus, giving the national Tea Party movement both political strength and clear leadership.

We both knew this was critical for the long-term goal of securing the House and Senate for generations to come. We knew that if we wanted "true conservatives" who were actually electable and would not manufacture campaign ads that said "raped women would not get pregnant," we needed heavyweight political operatives to join the movement.

At this time, the Tea Party and all her various factions were still not being taken seriously, and to some degree, this still holds true today. The Tea Party to actually become a serious power-broker must be taken seriously by the Republican Party and all of Washington, D.C. While 2010 had been successful, in all reality, 2010 had been somewhat of a stroke of luck and the conservatives who were elected, were thrust into office more off of "rebellious" vote or an "anyone but" vote rather than as a professionally organized "ballot box coup d'état.

The bottom line was, we had Tea Party groups in Iowa for instance that supported one candidate for Congress, while, up the street in another town, we had another group supporting a different candidate – all in the same district! This issue was not just relegated to Iowa; it was transpiring nationwide.

Why?

You are now beginning to see the concern that Charlie and I had for both the restoration of America and the survivability and growth of the Tea Party. For the Tea Party to truly expand, remain healthy, and become something truly remarkable in American political history, it desperately needed direction and unification with leadership; otherwise, it would flounder as different sects shot each other in the foot and keep putting up idiots to run for office.

With these thoughts in mind, we decided to not just form *Tea Party of America* but do with such a splash that all the patriots nationwide would jump on board. Once we had the organization in place, the vision was to "select the proper candidates to support through a quality vetting system." Decide which races we actually could influence win in and decide which candidates to back in those races. This was to be a professionally run organization. Now for the splash!

Think back in your memory banks for a moment and you will remember that in 2011, the political talk of the land was, *"will she or won't she?"* Almost every political talk program you turned your television to begged the question, *"Will Sarah Palin or Won't Sarah Palin run for President?"*

Iowa being the "First in the Nation" is nearly always the magnet that candidates flock to begin "testing the waters" for a potential run at the White House. This is the state where a potential candidate will come and literally spend a year (long before they announce) visiting those tractor dealerships, speaking at Rotary meetings, Lions Clubs, and county Republican Party meetings. This is how they begin setting up their campaigns, finding out if anyone is interested in what they have to say, and determining if there might be any support for their respective campaigns.

Sarah Palin being the "rock star" she had become, was not like the other candidates. Had she pulled into a Pizza Ranch to give a stump speech, it would have caused pandemonium in a small town. She simply couldn't take the same approach as the others. It is one thing to be a Governor of South Dakota whom nobody has heard of; it is quite another to be Sarah Palin with nearly 100% name recognition and 110% celebrity status.

Charlie and I knew that Governor Palin was "tossing" around the idea of making a run (or, at least, she had sent out the trial balloons) and we knew that we wanted a "monster rally event." We also knew that holding this event in the first week of September of 2011 was the perfect timing to attract the attention of the Governor to make a possible announcement that would shake the political foundations of the Republican Party to its core. All we needed now was the Former Governor of the Great State of Alaska to notice us and agree to speak. No problem, right?

Wrong!

Charlie and I were about to become involved in the perfect financial and political storm. How much of it was our own creation and how much of it was the creation of our own "in-house Satan, Craig" is a question we are still asking ourselves to this day.

We still had not a clue about Craig's real motivation or the utter deceitfulness of some operatives, but we were about to find out. Combine this with a Diva, the Diva's operatives, secrecy (yes almost straight out of a spy movie), a fledgling wannabe politician, an unscheduled rain shower, $75,000.00, two political rookies, naïve

Tea Party Patriots, every major news source on three continents, and some guy named Peter (with his own agenda), and you now have the ingredients for the perfect disastrous and embarrassing storm. By the way, does anyone know the definition of the term "bucolic?"

LET'S PARTY IN THE DESERT AND D.C.?

March 27, 2010, found tens of thousands gathering in the small Southern Nevada town known as Searchlight. Former Vice-Presidential candidate Sarah Palin had recently written in her bestselling book *Going Rogue* that her running partner Senator John McCain's handlers had put a leash on her regarding what she could and could not say during the 2008 campaign. By March of 2010, the leash was off; former Governor Sarah Palin was free to speak her mind – and speak she did!

By this time, she had become somewhat of a spiritual leader for the Tea Party world at large. She had spoken at several previous events where the crowds stood and cheered until they could not cheer any longer. She gave voice to their collective frustrations with vigor and passion. If Sarah Palin was not a superstar during the campaign, she certainly was now.

The organization known as Tea Party Express had their customized bus pointed toward Searchlight with Tea Party heroine Sarah Palin in tow. Founder Amy Kremer had decided on the Nevada town because it was the hometown to Tea Party villain, Senate Majority Leader

Harry Reid. While initially it seemed like a great idea to hold a rally in the middle of the Nevada desert, in hindsight it seems more like *Maybe we should have gone to the Rose Bowl instead?*

With only 1,000 residents and a location on a two-lane highway an hour from Las Vegas and about five hours from Los Angeles, Searchlight's facilities posed a significant issue. Between these metropolitan areas, there are some 10 million people to draw from. Surely if you hosted an event in a location with 10-plus million – not to mention those who could easily travel from Phoenix, Palm Springs, Reno and other major metro areas – you might just draw a crowd.

Although aerial photographs on the internet showed traffic backed up for miles and miles a full one-and-a-half hours after the program had begun, the liberal media claimed that only 5,000 people attended the rally. Actual estimates put the number into the tens of thousands of pitched tents, lawn chairs, and toted coolers into the rally site. The faithful who showed up that day were not let down; many conservative speakers gave them their best. While the original purpose of the rally was to inform Senator Reid that America did not want his and House Speaker Nancy Pelosi's "Affordable Care Act" aka, Obamacare, what began as a protest against this legislation soon became a full-scale assault on the handling of America by Barack Obama.

From a make-shift stage and speaker system, the patriot orators had the crowd vocalizing their universal dislike for the Obama administration. By the time our Tea Party superstar Palin hit the stage, the scene was reminiscent of when the Beatles arrived at Shea Stadium. The crowd was in a frenzy screaming for the new conservative rock-star. License plates could be seen from Kansas, Texas, Colorado, Oregon, Washington and even Mississippi. Governor Palin stood and delivered for the thousands who gathered in Searchlight, blasting Pelosi and Reid with patriotic rhetoric and assaulting their prized piece of legislation like a ravenous pack of wolves going after a sheep. Then she got down to business on the President's handling of taxes, jobs, defense, and domestic policy. Barack Obama's entire administration performance was in her crosshairs for targeting. And she did, in fact, shoot straight, metaphorically speaking. Sarah Palin rocked the house that day, to borrow an analogy from the younger crowd.

The year before, in 2009, radio and television personality Glenn Beck formed his 9-12 project. He was now ready to take it to the streets. By August of 2010, he had gathered many of his faithful in Washington, D.C. To date, Beck is without question the producer of the largest Tea Party rally in American history. That warm August day in D.C. brought out hundreds of thousands to hear Glenn, Governor Sarah Palin, and many more talk about long-standing American values.

It is widely accepted that the event in Searchlight, Nevada and Glenn Beck's Restoring Honor rally in D.C., were the most likely causes for the sweeping defeat of the Democrats in the midterm elections later that fall. These two events had motivated millions to hit the streets of America as a "Grassroots Ground Army" to support the many Tea Party-esque candidates campaigning for office.

By the fall of 2010, most American neighborhoods saw their front doors knocked on by more campaign volunteers than in any election in recent memory. Candidates like Pat Toomey, Ron Johnson, Nicky Haley, and Rand Paul were now becoming household names. They were rapidly beginning to frighten the hell out of the 'old-guard' in the hallowed halls of the political establishment's ivory towers.

In Wisconsin, newcomer Ron Johnson upset the Democrat power-broker Russ Feingold (Wisconsin) in probably one of the biggest shockers of that election's evening, when the results came pouring in. This simply wasn't supposed to happen. Wisconsin is typically a blue-collar, union card-carrying, and Democrat-supporting stronghold. What happened? How did a political novice businessman upset an entrenched Democrat United States Senator with the backing of the unions in a Union state?

Tea Party activist Mark Block is what happened. The mid-term elections of 2010 are what made Mark Block a Tea Party household name, but he had actually begun earning his Tea Party chops a couple of years earlier in Wisconsin – not without much controversy.

In 2001, Block had settled with the Wisconsin Election Board, paid a $15,000.00 fine for alleged campaign finance improprieties involving a 1997 election campaign of a State Supreme Court Judge. Block also agreed not to work in campaign finance positions until 2004 as part of the agreement to avoid prosecution.

Block was not to be relegated to the sidelines for long. A few years later he came back swinging for the fences when he was appointed to be the Director of the conservative pro-business organization Americans for Prosperity (AFP) for Wisconsin. From 2007 (when he went to work for AFP) through 2008 and into 2009, Block had turned AFP into a political machine and campaigning powerhouse. The interesting part of this story was that few really understood the depths of Mark Block's political muscle until *David defeated Goliath* on that cold November night of 2010.

Mark Block had indeed shocked, stunned (and several more redundant adjectives to make my point) and sent establishment Republicans to the Emergency Room with sudden attacks of angina. At that moment, the world took notice of Americans for Prosperity, and their vast political muscle would be felt far and wide in the coming years.

Though Mark Block does have a somewhat "controversial" background, the *Guru of the Grassroots* had rewritten the instructional manual for *how to win* with a ground game. In fact, in the coming years, AFP began spreading like wildfire across America. What once was a fairly localized lobbying group (for pro-business issues) was now raising vast amounts of cash; opening offices; hiring state directors with complete staffs in addition to field directors; recruiting volunteers (which were mostly Tea Party activists), and holding and sponsoring Tea Party rallies. Much of this success can be directly traced back to Mark Block.

As I said, Block did not come without controversy. Somewhere along the way (according to several good friends who have known Block personally for years), Mark apparently met a desk clerk at a Wisconsin hotel by the name of Linda Hansen. Much has been rumored for years in Tea Party circles about how this relationship began and how far it went. Close friends have told me that they have seen Block and Hansen entering hotel rooms at major rally events only to re-emerge hours later with their hair mussed up, makeup askew, and looking as though they had been wrestling.

I bring up this sordid little tale because not long after that Block took over the reins of the Herman Cain Presidential Campaign and appointed this "desk clerk" as Deputy Chief of Staff on a major Presidential campaign bid. Yes, you read correctly: Mark Block and Linda Hansen were managing a campaign for a notable business figure in America whom they had talked into running for President of the United States.

Conventional wisdom recognizes that a candidate must have faith in their team and particularly their manager. The nuclear radiation that someone of Mark Block's stature brought to the Cain campaign is the perfect example of the Tea Party's inability to select quality candidates. For someone of Cain's popularity to bring in someone as potentially toxic as Block was nothing short of political suicide. Again, hindsight is always 20/20, but this debacle could be seen miles ahead of time had someone taken their rose- colored glasses off.

Herman Cain ended up being just another strike against the Tea Party overall because it was the Tea Party who was "all in" for Herman and the infamous 999 plan.

SEVEN

SAY IT AIN'T SO: SARAH IS A DIVA?

The Merriam-Webster dictionary defines "bucolic" as "*of or relating to the country or country life.*"

The state of Iowa, with its beautiful rolling fields of corn blowing gently in the summer breeze, would, of course, fit the classic definition of the term bucolic. Lest you think Iowa is just a flat piece of ground with nothing other than telephone poles to view while driving across its length, you would, in fact, be mistaken. Iowa is the classic example of a Normal Rockwell painting. Many farms have the big, beautiful, two-story white homes with matching barns and a John Deere tractor sitting out front. In every aspect, *The Hawkeye State* exemplifies bucolic.

Not to put too fine of a point on it, but it is best described by famous actor Kevin Costner in the movie *Field of Dreams*. One day while Kevin's character is playing baseball in his youth, his father comes walking out of the field of corn for the first time, looks at his son, and inquires "Is this heaven?" Young Kevin's response? "No, this is Iowa." When a fellow can walk out of heaven and onto a ballfield in northeastern Iowa and mistake the state for heaven, it gives you a pretty clear indication of how its residents feel. OK, I know, this is a stretch, but it is actually relevant, so please bear with me.

My first foray into a living experience of the eloquent English word "bucolic" came during a phone call with one of Governor Palin's operatives.

It had been a long, hard fight to finally reach the point where I could speak to an actual living and breathing *somebody* who could provide solid answers regarding the Governor's appearance at our *Restoring America Rally* to be held on September 3, 2011.

As the rally's organizers, our entire goal was to introduce *Tea Party of America* (TPOA) to the American people in a large way. The process began with the introduction of TPOA, then moved into a recruitment effort in an attempt to unify the grassroots into a powerful voting bloc to begin the restoration process of our nation.

To make this happen, we needed a "superstar" in the Tea Party movement to make an appearance and attract coverage on national television; in essence, we needed Sarah Palin.

By this time, Governor Palin had indeed emerged as a superstar on several levels. She was, without question, the Tea Party darling and a political powerhouse. Palin had not just become the voice of the millions upon millions of oppressed conservatives, but she had also become emblematic of what we sought in a candidate. We judged our candidates according to the criteria of a "Palin Meter." How closely did candidate Ralph line up with Palin's belief system and how often did he use Palin buzzwords in his speeches?

Needless to say, at this point Sarah Palin was in high demand as a speaker, having just come off stellar appearances in Searchlight, Nevada, and Washington, D. C. at Glenn Beck's Restoring Honor event, plus countless others. Orchestrated by the national Tea Party Express group, Searchlight had been a monumental success. As a matter of fact, Searchlight had attracted national attention primarily because of its locale and the fact that this group of political misfits had managed to attract tens-of-thousands of people to a one-horse town with a population of only 1000 – and 100 miles from the nearest city.

In Washington D.C., Glenn Beck, tapping into his platform and prowess on Fox News, managed to bring together some 250,000 adoring patriots whom Beck and Palin rewarded with passionate speeches. To this day, people still talk about that event.

Despite her ability to draw huge crowds, Palin did come with a bit of a risk as well. With her career in full swing, she was now garnering upwards of $100,000.00 for an appearance. Charlie and I decided to go for broke and see if we could "sweet talk" her into appearing with us in exchange for footing the bill for a couple of plane tickets and a hotel room. (Hey, there's nothing wrong with dreaming big).

A man named Peter, whose last name I'll refrain from mentioning for reasons which will become obvious, was about to enter our lives while we prepared for this event. Charlie, Craig and I had begun planning in early spring when we sent an email to Governor Palin through her website. Months went by, with no response.

We'd originally decided that the least expensive venue for the Restoring America Rally would be the Wells Fargo Arena in downtown Des Moines. Hosting it there would have made it easy to control costs; without a doubt, it would have made the most sense from a financial standpoint.

By the time June rolled around, we were all but in a panic: no word still from Palin and no way to contact her except through her website email, which apparently nobody monitored (or, at least, we didn't think so).

Somewhere, somehow, one of the folks involved with the event had run across a fellow named Peter. Peter, as it turned out, was on a one-man mission to draft Sarah Palin to run for the 2012 nomination. So committed was this fellow to the cause, he had temporarily relocated from Los Angeles, California, where he was a fairly successful attorney, in order to dedicate a year of his income and time to garner enough excitement to compel Sarah into throw her hat into the ring and become an actual candidate.

The first time I met Peter, I received nothing short of a one-hour dissertation on why Sarah Palin was the only person on earth who could save and restore not just our nation, but the entire Universe. I couldn't determine if Peter was a groupie or fan, or totally obsessed with Governor Palin. It was almost frightening to watch his eyes when he spoke of her; there is not a dog on Planet Earth who has more affection in their eyes than Peter had when describing Sarah Palin and why she should be President.

After I had explained my plight to Peter during our initial meeting, he agreed to call his contact within the Palin inner circle. It turns out that Palin does, in fact, have an inner circle – a compact team that serves as her "insulation" against the outside world. She actually has professional politico types who advise her on if she should respond to this or that, or make a statement, or publish a blog, or whatever the case may be. Remember it is only Palin's thoughts on subjects that keep her relevant at this time in her career. She is no longer an elected official, nor is she a vice-presidential candidate. In order to earn money, she must stay popular and keep her name relevant in the political arena.

It is her staff of about five or six that manage her and her SuperPAC (Sarah PAC) while keeping her in the national spotlight. Just in case you doubt that these folks know what they're doing, take a quick look at these statistics.

In the 2010 midterm races (the election where the GOP trounced the Dems and retook the House of Representatives), Sarah Palin endorsed some 73 candidates. Of those 73, upon endorsement, nearly all were behind in the polls with only weeks left to go before the election. When the smoke cleared on election night, 71% or 52 of these underdogs had won their respective races. I cannot begin to tell you how ridiculously powerful this is in politics – Sarah simply showing up, holding someone's arm in the air, and uttering the words, "Please join me in supporting Bill Smith." She had truly become a 110-pound gorilla with extremely long coattails who was now officially scaring the stuffing out of the Republican Party. Nobody in history had been able to do what she had just accomplished.

With this sort of star power, what we in effect, were trying to accomplish was to convince the Rolling Stones to play my son's senior prom and not pay them for doing it. No problem, right?

After I had fully explained our fanciful dream to Peter, he assured me he would do his best to help us out. We were running out of time for organizing the event and certainly for reserving our accommodations.

After some two weeks of nail biting, praying, and becoming increasingly grumpy, we got the phone call – SARAH PALIN WAS IN and wanted to speak at the Restoring America Rally! The best part? She was "free" and did not even want a plane ticket or a hotel room. Honest to God, you could have knocked me over with a feather while I was on the phone with Peter. However (yes, there always seems to be a "however"), *Sarah wants bucolic!* She wants what? This was when I learned the definition of the word; Sarah wants a beautiful, bucolic backdrop.

Charlie and I looked at each other with no words spoken, but we knew we were both thinking the same thing. *Where the heck are we going to find a beautiful, bucolic backdrop for our Alaskan Diva? Furthermore, where are we going to find a backdrop that doesn't cost an arm and a leg, plus our first-born children?*

As we'd later discover, bucolic was to be just one of multiple demands Peter would be placing upon us.

Remember, we did not know Peter; all we knew was that he was the only one we could turn to who had a direct link to the Governor herself. When we began inquiring as to what else the governor needed or required for her appearance, we started receiving an exceptionally long list.

Each one of our Diva's demands seemed to cost more and more money. She wanted a stage (now this is where it get's tricky) only we were told, "*Ken, this is your event. The Governor will stand on a bail of hay if need be,*" but "*if you can come up with a nice stage, that would certainly be more preferable.*"

Wells Fargo Arena had included in their pricing the correct size staging, the correct sound systems, restrooms, concession stands, power and roof (this becomes relevant later) all of which we were going to have to contract for from an outside source.

In one phone call from Peter, we had gone from elation to "Oh crap, how in the world are we going to pull this off?" We had to fulfill a seemingly endless list of requirements to host thousands of people, plus the land, and lastly, security! *Security? Seriously?*

Oh yes, Peter went on to describe how the Governor receives more death threats than Barack Obama. When I questioned the rationale of this statement, he launched into an almost protective explanation about the extent of her popularity on the Right, and the utter fear it generated on the Left (a.k.a., Democrats), which resulted in daily death threats that demanded highly trained security.

My response was, "What is the possibility of actually speaking with her team Peter?" He then informed us in no uncertain terms that we must deal with Peter and Peter alone if we were to obtain Governor Palin. He expressed himself in delicate legalese, not in a threatening manner, but in the style of a highly skilled attorney who left no doubt as to his implications. In effect, he noted (and I am paraphrasing), "Hey, guys, you can deal with me on this or we can let you sink, with no Palin." It was at this moment that we began questioning Peter's end-game in all this.

Charlie and I miraculously (yes insert sarcasm here) had Craig chirping in our ears the entire time. Once it was determined we had to be "bucolic," Craig, of course, leaped into action. He had "friends" who would "cut us the good brother-in-law" deals on staging, sound systems, lighting, concessions and whatever else we might need. Craig instantly became the lead production counselor of sorts in all of this.

We decided to begin assigning duties because we needed a large team yesterday if we were going to pull this off successfully. One nice thing about Charlie being the leader of the Des Moines Tea Party was that we had a built-in volunteer pool to assist. Craig did become the defacto production leader and assembled a competent team to begin handling details. In retrospect, this was something akin to putting the fox in charge of the hen house; the only problem was, we did not know it at the time.

Charlie and I were somewhat stumped as to how much all this was going to cost. When we mentioned our concern to Craig, he promptly informed us, "Oh don't worry about it; we can get AFP (Americans For Prosperity) to pay for some of this and we can get the NRA (National Rifle Association) to write a big check also."

If one is going to hold a majorly successful event, one must start marketing it early on. And by early on, I mean months in advance. The sooner you start marketing, the bigger the crowd because (and this is particularly true in the Tea Party Nation) people will actually make plans and come from distant places if they have enough notice.

Charlie and I were already making plans on the specifics of how to market this monumental event with our stated goal of tens of thousands of attendees when the phone call came down from on high.

"By the way guys," Peter began, "I forgot to tell you, *this is to be kept top-secret, Palin doesn't want her name attached to this yet. We must keep it hush, hush."*

Just when we did not think the day could get any worse, it did.

EIGHT

DO WE PARTY WITH TRACTORS OR BALLOONS?

No pressure, none, I feel great!

This is what I kept telling myself as I walked up and down the hills of a historic tractor farm just 15 miles west of Des Moines. Believe it or not, a group of farmers created something akin to a hall of fame for tractors; a beautiful site with rolling hills and large trees. The museum portion sits in a huge barn on a perch overlooking Interstate 80 and the distant hills, where the corn blows in the wind. The scene was most definitely "bucolic," as our Alaskan Diva had requested.

With it now being June and still no site having been located for the event, yes, I was feeling the pressure. Money was being invested, our Diva had committed, and the word was leaking out that *she* was coming to town. Add to the mix the copious amount of pressure I was feeling from Tea Party organizations across America to pull this off, and you can imagine how I felt. Remember, having Sarah Palin speak at a major event is tantamount to holding a conservative political Super Bowl for folks who wave "snake flags."

While I was busy researching sites for the event, Charlie handled the cash flow and Craig managed the volunteers who had committed to assisting us. He'd wrangled about a dozen unpaid workers who were willing to invest their time, energy, and even a small amount of their financial resources. Thankfully, one particular gentleman was a civil engineer (which it turns out we needed) who took aerial photos of the site to estimate the permissible amount of cars that could be parked on the day of the rally.

After having walked the first site (the tractor museum) and blueprinted parking, we determined the terrain just would not work; if it happened to rain a day or two prior – or worse yet on rally day, we could be in serious trouble. The parking area would have become impassable for cars to get in and out. If you were not in a 4x4 truck, basically you'd be stuck. Combine the parking issue with security (according to Peter's dictates) and this site simply was not going to work.

Nevertheless, Charlie and I liked the location, mainly because it of the cost. The folks who owned it were going to allow us to rent the facility for a nominal fee of $2,500 for the day. They even promised to groom the site. Truly, it was a lovely location with easy access off the freeway, trees to shade the party-goers, and a small hill in which to place the staging. But alas, we simply could not take the chance of having 2,000 cars stuck in the mud if the worst case scenario transpired. In the end, we'd be thanking our stars we decided to change locations.

For now, it was off to do more scouting.

The year prior, I had attended our annual balloon festival, which had been hosted on a site with gravel parking that could accommodate thousands of cars with controlled entrances. It had the bucolic backdrop for the Diva, and a gentle hill where thousands upon thousands could either sit in chairs or on the grass. It was designed like something along the lines of a natural amphitheater. The site also had small buildings which had been used as concession stands during the balloon festival and was exposed nicely for security purposes (per Peter). We might just have something here!

We held a meeting at the site with Charlie, Craig, the security committee, the volunteers, and me. Our volunteers were in charge of everything from food to porta potties. Yes, we had a committee for every item we felt we would need; we even had someone in charge of contracting with Sam's Club for ice.

Somewhere in the middle of our meeting (where we actually walked around and discussed all the potential issues and needs), it was decided that the little platform at the bottom of the hill would not work. WE NEEDED STAGING! I, for one, was not so sure and neither was Charlie, but Peter decided we had to have the correct lighting to put this event on television.

Did I just say television? Yes, it was determined around the first of July that this event was actually newsworthy because this was Iowa, where candidates were beginning to campaign – and Sarah Palin was a potential candidate. Would she actually announce at our event? Could it be that we would be part of presidential history? These were now the rumors flying across the bucolic skies of The Hawkeye State.

If this was actually going to hit the airwaves, Peter demanded that the staging reflect the stature of such a candidate. Don't forget, he was also obsessed with Palin on an emotional level. In Peter's world, Palin walked on political water. Also, remember that Peter was our only conduit to the Palin camp; there was zero way to verify any of the demands he placed on us.

Now Craig and Peter were at the bottom of the hill discussing staging. Miraculously, Craig just happened to have a friend from Cedar Falls or Cedar Rapids or Cedar-something who owned a company that sold, rented, and constructed professional staging. "Praise be to the Lord," this was covered! (Yes, that was tongue-in-cheek).

Keep in mind this is supposed to be a rally that lasts about three hours. It is now being decided by our two "rocket scientists" that the stage must be some 40 feet wide and about 20 feet deep. It needs to have an awning over it with banks of lights which can be controlled from a panel behind the stage, or out in the center of the crowd. Good old Craig could handle this with no problem.

Charlie and I met the next morning with the folks who owned the balloon field. They politely informed us that for an affordable sum of only $10,000 we too could rent this field. Yes, you read correctly – only $10,000 to rent a bucolic site for our Diva, one we're going to use for less than one day.

Basically, what was happening was that some naïve Tea Party folks were being used for a politically charged and crafted public relations stunt to promote a superstar and whatever she was cooking up next. Only we did not know it at the time.

Every time Charlie or I questioned Craig about the status of AFP or the NRA, he told us, "Oh, I'm just waiting to hear back from them, but all is good." With this carrot dangling above our heads, the $10,000 dagger didn't seem quite so sharp.

Ulimately, we made the deposits for the site, confirmed the Diva's appearance, priced out porta-potties, contracted concessions with the same supplier that takes care of the State Fair of Iowa (now everyone can have a corn dog) and put our marketing plan in place (that we cannot use because of Peter's instructions). What could possibly go wrong now?

Craig is what could go wrong. His "brother-in-law" deal for staging was about to come home and it was going to send reverberating shock waves across those beautiful bucolic fields of Iowa.

One day, he phoned in one of his typical "all is good" tones and summarily informs us that for only $25,000 we can rent the necessary staging, sound systems, and lighting.

Combine this with $10,000 for the balloon field, $4,000 for the backdrop screen, $10, 000 more for tee-shirts, tens of thousands more for many other miscellaneous items, and we now officially had a $75,000 production.

The once proud Tea Party flag-waving patriots had now been reduced to panic-stricken Patriots on a mission. Charlie and I both agreed at breakfast one July morning that we simply could not allow this event to fail – somehow it had to work!

It was then that we both agreed to do something out of the norm. We decided to charge $5 for parking and price the tee-shirts at $20. Theoretically, between the parking, shirts, and concessions, we should be able to cover our costs. If Craig comes through with some cash from the NRA or Americans For Prosperity, then we should actually be in a profit situation.

All was rocking along pretty well as Charlie had decided to cover the cost up-front with the understanding he would be paid back after the event. Meetings were held almost daily at this point amongst the event staff and Craig was doing a great job of getting everything sorted out.

Around the first of August, Peter informed us that our "security" needed to be laid out for the Governor. We were told she was getting more death threats than Barack Obama himself. Now I am not one who usually conveys a "deer in the headlights" look, but I am pretty certain in that moment I had that look on my face. I know Charlie did.

As we sat at our corner booth drinking coffee with the phone on the table and the speaker spewing this latest round of bad news, all Charlie and I could do was put our heads in our hands and ask "What next?" Peter went on to inform us that the security could not be comprised of regular police officers; these guys needed to be Secret Service caliber of agents who are pros at this sort of thing.

After hanging up with Peter, Charlie and I stared out the window of the Village Inn for probably 10 minutes before either of us spoke.

Charlie in his wisdom asked, "Do you think this is real?" I replied, "I have heard she does get a ton of threats, but the seriousness of them, I honestly don't know Charlie." However, none of that mattered: we were told by the official *PALINISTA* that she had to have presidential-like security.

A few days later, we were back at the balloon field with a Secret Service-approved security agency. I never realized that agencies actually sought this coveted endorsement because when dignitaries showed up and the Secret Service needed extra help, they would call on these agencies to assist. I later found out that many of the employees at this level were ex-Seals, Green Berets, and Black Water types of guys. In other words, these fellows are not folks anyone wants to mess with.

As we walked the grounds, our security official told us not to worry about that tree line because they would have someone patrolling over there, and not to worry about the parking lot as they would have a fellow out there with a dog that sniffed for bombs. Charlie and I listened and shook our heads the entire time. Still, we were doing pretty well until he got to the part where they were going to have a sniper in a helicopter circling overhead.

Throughout the conversation, Palinista Peter nodded his head in approval of the security fellow's recommendations.

When the smoke cleared, it was agreed that she would have four body men as they are titled. She would have a parameter of eight more scattered around the staging area and yet another eight working the parking lot, tree line, and concession area. YES, Sarah Palin was getting 20 security guards and a helicopter with a sniper for her security.

And all for the nominal fee of somewhere around $12,000. We were about to shell out another $12 grand; that is until we received phone call number one.

Once again at breakfast (at our unofficial office and in our corner booth) about three weeks out from the rally, we received a phone call from someone in Indiana. The exchange went something like this:

"Hi, is this Ken Crow?"

"Yes, it is, whom may I ask is calling?"

"This is "Jim" and I work for Sarah Palin!" (name is changed for his protection)

Really, was my response. He went on to inform me he was just touching base to inquire as to how everything was coming along and to let me know the Governor was excited to be coming back to Iowa and, in fact, would be in town for the Iowa Fair in a few days. I gave Jim the update that everything was going according to schedule and told him about the staging, the promotion, and the site, running down my whole list. It was when I came to the security portion that someone had to pull me down from the ceiling.

Jim began asking questions about "someone" named Peter. I said, "Yes, he has been helping us ensure the event meets Governor Palin's specifications." To which Jim unceremoniously informed me, "Peter doesn't speak for the Governor or her staff!" When I repeated his words aloud so Charlie would know what was happening, he almost gagged on his coffee.

"So let me get this straight: this guy who purports to speak for the Governor, but in fact, *doesn't* speak for the Governor, just had us spend $25,000 on a stage so she would be properly showcased for national television. Do you mean to tell me to tell me, you guys knew nothing of this?"

"Oh, yes, we knew, he kept us informed, but you don't have to do that if you can't afford it."

Believe it or not, I'm still holding it together pretty well until he got to the now infamous line, "*Ken, it is you guys's rally, you can do whatever you like, the Governor will be just as happy speaking while standing on a hay bail!"*

It was at this point, I wanted to kill something; that something was Peter. Jim must have sensed my unbridled anger because he launched into a dissertation about how grateful the Governor would be for our graciousness and how spectacular the production would be with the staging.

It was then that he inquired about security. I proudly told him about the 20 agents and even the helicopter. That's when he proceeded to not just chuckle but openly laugh out loud! Charlie and I should have sensed something was going on, but the truth was, we just did not know better. We had no idea of the level of deceit, corruption, or outright dishonesty transpiring within our beloved Tea Party. We genuinely believed these were all good people simply trying to save our nation. The soon-to-emerge truth would tell a much different story, one with ramifications we're still suffering from, nearly five years later.

We were about to get the second phone call!

Sarah Palin's bus at Restoring America Rally, September 3, 2011 in Indianola Iowa.

Ken speaking at Restoring America Rally, September 3, 2011 in Indianola Iowa.

Ken with Sarah Palin at Restoring America Rally, September 3, 2011 in Indianola Iowa.

Sarah Palin speaking at Restoring America Rally, September 3, 2011 in Indianola Iowa. (below)

Searchlight Nevada Tea Party event on March 27, 2010.

Jenny Beth Martin and Mark Mecklenberg.

Amy Kremer.

Deborah Johns.

2014 PAC Summary Data

Select a Cycle: 2014

Total Receipts	$14,376,069
Total Spent	$14,207,746
Begin Cash on Hand	$0
End Cash on Hand	$168,323
Debts	$0
Independent Expenditures	$1,418,695
Date of last report	December 31, 2014

2014 PAC Contribution Data

Contributions from this PAC to federal candidates (list recipients)	$0
Contributions to this PAC from individual donors of $200 or more (list donors)	$3,357,271

Official PAC Name:
TEA PARTY PATRIOTS CITIZENS FUND
Location: WOODSTOCK, GA 30189
Industry: Republican/Conservative
Treasurer: PAUL KILGORE
FEC Committee ID: C00540898
(Look up actual documents filed at the FEC)

Money raised and spent on candidates by Tea Party Patriots Citizens Fund. Image courtesy of Open Secrets.

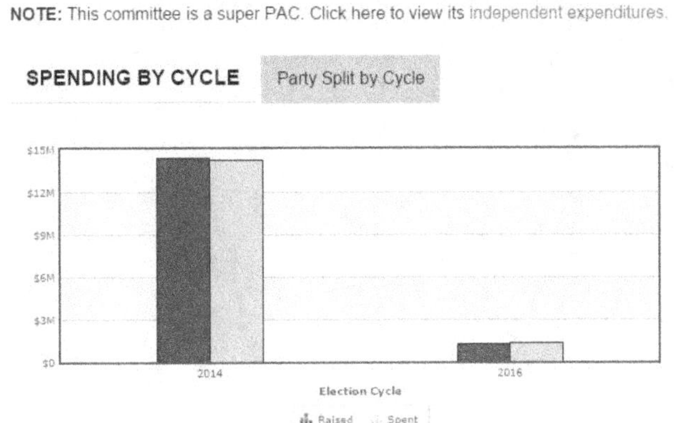

Money raised and spent on candidates by Tea Party Patriots Citizens Fund, 2014 vs. 2016. Image courtesy of Open Secrets.

NINE

YES, VIRGINIA, A PHONE CALL CAN CHANGE EVERYTHING

As Jim continued his uncontrollable laughter, I placed the phone on the table and clicked on the speaker. "Jim, Jim, come on Jim," I pleaded until I finally heard a sniff, followed by his oh so politically correct language.

"Ken, we will provide security, you guys are not responsible for that at all."

"*What?*"

"Yeah, no problem," he said. "Governor Palin has her own security and who told you that you needed to provide that anyway?"

"Peter!" I screamed at the phone.

The truth was out: we could have scaled this thing back significantly had Peter not been involved. Jim then told us "not listen" to Peter any longer regarding the organizing of this event. He reiterated, "Ken, this is you guys' event, you handle it any way you want, the Governor is just proud to be showing up."

However, the checks had already been written and cashed for much of the setup.

After hanging up, Charlie and I were once again, two deer in the headlights. Over the past two months, we had been doing exactly what Peter told us to do, primarily because we could not talk with the Palin camp to determine her plans as to whether she would show up or not. We had no idea about her requirements in exchange for an appearance, much less what type of staging or anything else for that matter. Now we found out we were heavily invested to the tune of about $40,000 in an event which held no promise of breaking even and might even lose money for us.

At this point, I called Jim back and inquired, "Jim, if I can get our money back for the balloon field, can we move this thing inside to the arena in downtown Des Moines?"

He politely informed me that "it was our event and we could do whatever we liked, except the Governor was really looking forward to a bucolic (there was that word again) setting from which to give her very important address." *Very important address, did he just say a very important address to the nation? Yes, he had indeed said those magic words!*

Somewhere in this midst of the phone calls flying back and forth, we were also informed that C-SPAN, FOX News, and 78 more networks (yes, I am exaggerating, but not by much or, at least, it didn't seem by much) were going to carry this speech live, plus live stream it to the internet. What did they all know that we did not know? Of course, every time I inquired as to what the Governor's intentions were, I was told, "Only Todd (and maybe not even him) and the Governor herself know the answer to that."

At this point, we were still being held under the "tight-lipped" status, yet I was getting phone calls from networks wanting press credentials, nationally known bloggers, reporters from the networks, political pundits, and newspapers. All were coming to this event! It never occurred to me to ask, how did all these people get my cell number? But I didn't.

If this was not all strange enough, I got another phone call from Arizona, the one that would rock our world. Remember our beloved witch who wasn't a witch at all, but a Tea Party Diva in her own right? Yep, Christine O'Donnell was resurfacing!

The smooth, polite fellow on the other end of the phone asked if I was Ken Crow and of course, I said, yes. He then informed me he was calling on behalf of the Christine O' Donnell camp and was wondering if there might possibly be an open spot left in the speaking lineup?

After having just jumped through hoops for the Alaskan Diva crew, I knew better than to commit to accepting Christine O'Donnell without prior approval from the Governor herself.

The issue of putting two celebrity Divas on the same stage at the same event can be problematic at best. The Tea Party movement had already begun to create pseudo-celebrities of sorts and these individuals had egos the size of Texas.

I told Tim (the caller from Arizona) I needed to make a phone call and get clearance as I had already emailed the speaker lineup (or white sheet as it's known) to the Palin camp.

I called Jim back at Palin Central to inquire about the matter and he replied with, "No problem Ken, this is your event and you can have whomever you like. If you're asking if the Governor has an issue with Christine, no she doesn't. As a matter of fact, they often text each other and Sarah Palin even endorsed her when she ran for the Senate last year."

Smiling, I hung up the phone and looked at Charlie. We were both elated and displaying smug grins like two cats who had just caught two mice. This meant we could now have two superstars instead of just one, which in turn meant more coverage, more attendees, and yes, more revenue.

I returned Tim's call and gave him the good news that he could bring Christine; just tell her to leave her witch costume back in Delaware. We both chuckled and all was good for the rest of the day.

Almost simultaneously (we later learned, possibly a day ahead), the Palin crew had her at the State Fair and issued press releases about the upcoming event. Now the world knew. This was where her team had shot reels of video in which they were making an advertisement of Sarah mingling with happy fair-goers. She was even seen with the world-famous butter cow. The video was also interspersed with Sarah speaking in patriotic terms about America's potential and how much she believed in our people and how much she loved Iowa. Of course, the video ended with a giant Grizzly Bear roaring and pawing at the sky. By now Sarah was officially known as the Mama Grizzly.

As Charlie and I reviewed the white sheet about the best spot to insert O'Donnell into the itinerary, we began reflecting on just how far we had actually come.

What began as a conceptual idea to unify a movement to seize more political power nationally had now grown into an event of mammoth proportions. It was even going to even be televised nationally. Charlie and I were almost like proud parents watching their child swim or ride a bike for the first time. We were almost giddy with enthusiasm not just for the rally, but for "who" was going to be attending and speaking. In addition to Sarah and Christine, we lined up Dr. Sam Clovis (who today is presidential candidate Donald Trump's senior political adviser), Tony Katz (nationally syndicated conservative radio host), a host of other talent ranging from Gospel singers to a political comedian named Eric Golub from Los Angelos (this guy is hysterical by the way), and me. Yes indeed, this was not just your run-of-the-mill rally; this was an event of epic proportions for Iowa and everyone knew it.

But alas, as they say, "all good things must come to an end."

The next morning after our *happy time* at the Village Inn with all the good news, the phone rang at 7:00 a.m. sharp. This time, the call was from both Jim and Don from the Palin camp.

The first words out of their collective mouths were, "Ken, you have to cancel Christine now, you can't have her at the Restoring America event in Indianola, Iowa!" The excuse I was given was, "the blogosphere is blowing up this morning and it's not good".

I literally could not speak for the first few moments after the shell-shock I had just received. I had to call Charlie, and I had no idea what to do or say. I told the guys I would call them back shortly. They seemed to oblivious to my plight; they simply did not care. They both restated their position and then made it seem even more ominous by restating that "Christine could not come, I had to cancel her and it was non-negotiable."

I immediately called Charlie, who sounded much like Kermit the Frog. Charlie, it turned out, had had fallen prey to Montezuma's revenge or the flu or something, but the bottom line was, I was on my own for the next day or two as he was running a high fever and not doing well at all. *Could this possibly get any worse?*

I called the guys back and promised to cancel Christine O'Donnell. Almost immediately, I began receiving phone calls from most of the usual media sources. This wasn't a phone call every thirty minutes, this was a phone call on top of phone calls and then 30 more phones calls. Within an hour, I had my entire message center fill up and still the phone would not stop ringing.

The one commonality among every call was "Why are you canceling Christine O'Donnell?" And the tragedy was, I had no idea, other than the fact I was told to do so by Sarah Palin's handlers.

Since bed-ridden Charlie could barely talk, I had nobody to consult with on this except Craig. That's the answer: *Craig is an old political hack, he will know what to say to the press and how to handle this. I will call Craig!*

Well, Craig abruptly told me I had to be firm with the press and with the Palin folks as well. *Yeah, Craig, thanks for the help amigo.*

The next call I received was from the Alaskan Dispatch out of Anchorage. *You have to be kidding*, I thought to myself. The voice on the other end of the phone seemed to be almost soothing; she was polite and understanding and refrained from demanding answers. *Finally, a friendly voice*, I thought.

Up until this point, I had not really given a firm statement as to what had happened and why Christine was being canceled. As a matter of fact, it was now about 10:00 a.m. Central Time and I had not officially canceled Christine yet. The only contact I had for her was Tim, my new friend out in Phoenix, and I thought it was still a bit early to be dropping this bombshell.

Have you ever said something and as you're saying it, you are literally watching the words escape your lips while you're flailing at them and trying to reinsert them into your mouth? The entire time you're speaking, you're saying to yourself, *My God did I just say that, why, why did I just say that?*

The nice lady from the Anchorage newspaper had me and she knew it. When she asked, "*So, Ken, what really happened here, why did you cancel Christine, or was it that you were forced to cancel her?*" it immediately sent up a red flag. I knew if I told the truth, Sarah would cancel, the press would come down on her like a ton of bricks, and my name would be mud within the Tea Party community.

The words began leaving my lips and for a fleeting second, I thought this was the answer. "It's not their fault, it is totally my fault."

"*What do you mean Ken, it is your fault, what happened?*"

"Hey look, I am just a grassroots kind of guy and a dumb cowboy; this major rally organizing stuff is something I am not used to and I overbooked the speaking roster. Blame it all on me."

And blame they did!

I was now officially known as the dumb cowboy from coast to

coast; the stupid redneck who could not keep track of a schedule. What I had effectively done was fallen on my sword for both ladies and their respective contingents. Why? Why did I just ruin myself for years to come? This might have been the noble thing to do, but it certainly was not the smart thing to do if you wanted to go farther in this life.

The headlines on websites and even in newsprint led with "The self-described dumb cowboy" did this, said this, did that and has ended up eating Crow. In one fashion or another, the 24-hour news cycle (all because this involved Sarah Palin) was *Ken Crow is a dumb cowboy*. But the pain was not to end anytime soon.

My new friend Craig was about to take a dagger and run it in my back, only I didn't know it yet.

I made my phone call sometime just before 12:00 noon out to Phoenix and had that talk with Tim, who was reassuring and understanding. He seemed to sense something was wrong here, along with my utter desperation. I ended up talking with him for about an hour and discovered he was deeply involved in Tea Party activities in the Arizona area as well as nationwide. I also learned a great deal about how to deal with the press since he was in the media business himself. Tim, it turned out, owned a major Tea Party publication online and he'd organized several other major productions himself.

By mid-afternoon, I was now the laughing stock of the Tea Party world, while the ladies remained conspicuously quiet. They had both gone underground. By the 5:00 p.m. news nationwide, I had actually made the headlines of most major news outlets. I was now the punchline for many broadcasters' storylines about the big Sarah Palin event. Sarah was now the victim of bad organizing and Christine was the victim of a dumb cowboy.

The bottom line to the first day of the fiasco: I was being skewered in the media but tragically, I was totally innocent in all of it. Yet I was being destroyed on many levels, both professionally and personally.

However, what I experienced that first day was nothing compared to what was about to happen the second day. Some five years later, I'm still paying for the events that transpired on day two.

TEN

YOU BETCHA, THIS IS GETTING UGLY

I vividly remember my first night arriving in Chicago, Illinois for the United States Navy to attend basic training at the Great Lakes Training Center just north of Chicago.

As I was leaving my seat on the plane, I clutched my large tan folder as though I had a death grip on it. Exiting the aircraft, I looked around and remember thinking how utterly frightened I was because I had no idea where to go and furthermore, I had not a clue who to ask.

As I walked down the aisle, I happened to run across an MP (Military Police), all starched and pressed in his Marine Corps uniform and I must have looked pretty disheveled and lost. He noticed I had no luggage, no briefcase, and no obvious destination other than where I was supposed to be going.

"*HEY Sailor, are you heading to boot camp?*" he asked.

"Yes, I am," was my response.

He patiently pointed me in the right direction toward the front door, with the instructions to wait out front and a description of what my bus would look like. Totally consuming relief enveloped my soul.

That is until I walked out the front door to O'Hare Internation Airport and was hit in the face with snow and sub-zero temperatures when all I had on was a long-sleeved western shirt and a wind breaker. Between the heavy gusts, the body-numbing temperature and the snow burning my cheeks, I honestly thought I had just died and gone someplace highly undesirable.

I remember as I stood under the little awning at the bus stop I could not stop my uncontrollable shaking. I had been up since 4:00 a.m. that morning, taken the ASVAB battery exam, and been poked, prodded and had every orifice on my body examined at the recruiting center in Dallas, Texas. It was now 11:00 p.m. and here I am standing in a snowstorm in a strange city where I am totally alone, frightened, and freezing to death. I just wanted to go home!

As I was standing in my driveway after my phone had finally slowed down, I was trying desperately to think. Memories of my Chicago experience came flooding back because I now experienced those exact same feelings again. I was literally shivering in my driveway from anxiety and it was 85 degrees that summer night.

Just as I was about to officially begin my meltdown process, the phone rang. It was Craig. After the fake (which were supposed to be comforting) "how are you doing" pleasantries were out of the way, he began giving me political advice to overcome the daunting problem I was now facing.

He asked, "Ken, do you ever play poker?"

"Of course, I love to play hold-em."

He then launched into a speech about how I should shove my chips and challenge the Palin folks to regain control of the situation. By shoving my chips, he meant I should stand my ground by re-inviting Christine and forcing Sarah to back down. He swore on his mother's grave that they would acquiesce and agree to let O'Donnell appear along with Palin at the event. *"All-in"* became my mantra that night, and I got Tim back on the phone.

In his political wisdom, Tim repeatedly asked if I thought I was doing the right thing. "Of course, I am," I explained. "Our political guru Craig with the golden resume told me I should do this."

"What happens if the Palinista's don't go for this Ken"?

What Tim was trying to do in a delicate way was talk me off the cliff and keep me from jumping. Unfortunately, the dumb cowboy was not picking up on his wisdom and insisted anyway that Christine was re-invited. I was not going to be bullied and the chorus of "Hey Ken, this is your event," kept swimming in my mind.

Tim finally agreed to my demands and made the phone call. By now it was around 11:00 p.m. and everyone was exhausted. I called the Palin crew back and gave them the news. Their response sent shivers down my spine; I knew this was going to be an exceptionally long night.

At 7:00 the next morning, I received another phone call from the Palin boys. My worst fears had been realized and the phone started ringing again from the media. SARAH PALIN HAD BEEN PUT ON HOLD!

Without Palin, our event would have to be canceled as there would be no way it would be televised. There would be mediocre crowds at best and we would lose tens of thousands of dollars and the worst part was, I had just shoved my poker chip stack and did not just get called, but had been badly beaten in the hand.

I had to make another phone call, one that would prove to be my most humiliating to date. It turned out that Tim was expecting it and he remained comforting. Amazingly, he did not call me stupid, nor did he reaffirm the extent of my dire predicament, one of my own making. Instead, he remained totally polite, gracious, and understanding while informing me we needed to talk after the event was over.

Once the confirmation came that Christine was indeed canceled for the second time, the Palin crew did lift the "hold" on her appearance, but not before a now infamous article had been sent around the world for me to live with.

Iowa Tea Party rally organizer Ken Crow eats crow over Palin drama

Amanda Coyne
The New York Times
September 2, 2011

Editor's note: *Alaska Dispatch reporter Amanda Coyne is in Iowa reporting on Sarah Palin and her speech Saturday to the Iowa-based political action committee, the Tea Party of America PAC. Check back for updates on Palin Watch and Amanda's blog.*

DES MOINES -- The Iowa Republican, the go-to political website for Iowans, featured a piece this morning by the site's editor that said that Sarah Palin has no business running for president if she can't even pull off a speech in Iowa without drama, where Christine O'Donnell was invited to speak, then disinvited, then invited and disinvited again after Palin threatened to pull out of the event. Here's the nut:

If the drama surrounding the Tea Party of America event over the past few days has proved anything, it's that Sarah Palin is not ready to run for president. That's not to say that she will never run for president, but the events of the last few days have confirmed that Palin has not built the necessary political apparatus to effectively run for national office.

Ken Crow, from Tea Party of America, is one of the organizers of the event. He's the one who is taking responsibility for the Palin/O'Donnell drama. He told the Des Moines Register on Thursday, "I'm a political rookie. I'm the dumb cowboy. I've been a rodeo cowboy my whole life, and I don't know how to be anything different."

When I repeated the dumb cowboy line to Crow on the phone on Friday, he chuckled his best cowboy chuckle and said, "that's what I want people to think." Getting serious, he said the whole affair has been pretty brutal. He said that he's made apologies all around: to Christine O'Donnell -- who he said was very gracious -- to Sarah Palin's people. He will also apologize to Palin herself when he talks to her tomorrow.

One writer at Conservatives4Palin, however, doesn't seem to be accepting the whole dumb cowboy schtick. Stacy Drake, one of the site's regular contributors, wrote a piece on Wednesday entitled, "Why Did Ken Crow Make Such a Mess Out of the Iowa Rally?" The piece features a photo of Crow and GOP candidate Rick Perry talking. Drake, responding to other theories claiming that his might be all a big ruse by the Perry team to make Palin seem less than presidential, wrote that she doesn't believe that the Perry camp had been planning this for months, nor is she convinced that it came from his camp at all. However, she wrote:

I do know that Ken Crow is a Rick Perry supporter who has managed to make a mess out of a highly publicized event that Governor Palin will be headlining on Saturday. I also know that he has been trashing Governor Palin to the press.

Crow said has great respect for the C4Palin team, but that he doesn't respond to "idiocy or untruths." But then he did exactly that. For one, he said, he hasn't made up his mind who he is going to support and that he has spoken to Perry for only one minute in his entire life, and that was about Texas, the state that Crow is from and that Perry currently governs. The photo happened to be shot during that one minute at an Iowa GOP fundraiser in Des Moines when Perry man grabbed him on the shoulder.

Secondly, he has never, ever said anything derogatory about Palin. Not to family, friends, and certainly not to the media.

Crow was on his way to check out the scene in Indianola (where I'm heading momentarily). He said that it's already starting to fill up. Lawn chairs are going down on the grass in a field where it's been held tomorrow. He said that RVs are beginning to roll in, and that's he's continually receiving emails from people coming from all across the country. People who have worked overtime to save up enough money to come. People on fixed incomes. He expects the event to be a raging success.

"I've never seen anything like the love that people have for her," he said.

Contact Amanda Coyne at Amanda(at)alaskadispatch.com. Her views a*re her own.*

After dozens of radio and television interviews regarding the Christine and Sarah debacle, we still had no answer for $64,000 question: *Was Sarah Palin announcing her candidacy for the Presidency?* Up until the great rift, this had been the overriding theme of the event. Was Sarah announcing? Remember, this was the reason for the media hype in the first place.

The afternoon before the big announcement or rally or whatever this fiasco had turned into, I made my way out to the site. Low and behold, as I was arriving so was Sarah Palin's Mama Grizzly bus. The huge vehicle eased its way to a point on the hillside behind the stage, where the world and television cameras would certainly capture it in all its splendor.

When it parked, I was standing at the fence separating the crowd area from the stage. Two gentlemen walked up to me and introduced themselves. Wouldn't you know, they were our friends from the phone conversations – *Sarah's handlers, Don, and Jim!*

At this point that I had begun pondering, *"What if this entire fiasco portion had been a staged event?"*

I decided to test the water and see if my hypothesis might have any merit.

"So Don, I have just one thing to say to you," I stated.

"Oh yeah, what's that?"

I informed him that if I were 20 years younger, I would hop over the fence and whip his butt. His response stunned me to the point of disbelief.

"Yeah, Ken, but it got you $10,000,000 worth of free press for your event!"

Don had just confirmed my worst fears: the entire Christine O'Donnell episode had in fact been staged to accomplish two goals. The first to create "hype" for unearned media promotion purposes, and the second to deflect attention from whether Palin was actually going to toss her hat into the field of presidential candidates. Then there were other more nefarious aspects of what was happening that I still wasn't aware of – Craig and the dagger portion of this whole ordeal.

The sad truth was, Charlie and I had been "handled" effectively by the politically experienced team who worked for Sarah Palin. We had been used, abused, and totally trashed, all for political gamesmanship by Palin's political operatives.

They knew full well what we would do, how we would respond, and what we would say two steps and two days ahead of what we even knew we would say or do. They guys were good, *they were very good* and the more I thought about it and replayed it all in my mind, the angrier I became.

How did the media pick all of this up so rapidly, almost before we had hung up the phone on the first day? Palin had put out press releases. At this point in time, her media folks could put out a press release and with one keystroke, it went to tens of thousands of media sources in a millisecond.

How did Christine O'Donnell's people get mine and Charlie's cell phone numbers? Nobody had those numbers but our staff and, of course, the Palin camp. These were all questions that came flooding into my mind.

At every turn, press releases went out and when the reporters called, someone at the Palin camp said, "We don't know, you will have to ask Ken; here is his cell number."

The longer I thought about this, the sicker I became. My reputation had been destroyed, Charlie was about to lose a boatload of money and for what? All of this personal destruction to ensure Sarah Palin got free hype – free hype she didn't even need because she already possessed a huge fan base and was as popular as they come.

The one question about everything that transpired, I will never be able to answer is: *Did Sarah Palin know about this (what her operatives were doing) and if so, then how could you do this to somebody that you don't even know?*

This shady political maneuvering has wrought an untold amount of damage on me personally. When you Google my name today, the first two or three pages of articles are about this event and how badly it was handled. I wonder if Sarah Palin realizes that because of all this bad press, I am now unemployable? In our current high-tech society, nearly all major corporations Google potential employees to see what that potential hire has been up to for the last several years.

As I walked the field and the beautiful bucolic setting, the refrigerator trucks were pulling in and setting up, as were the concession stands to ensure everyone had plenty to eat. The tractor trailers were parked and the stage and sound crews were running tests. Charlie, who was feeling much better by now, set up his multiple boxes of tee-shirts. Many of the speakers were calling in to let us know they had safely arrived at their rooms.

Harlan, my guardian angel who had been by my side the entire time and even through the disaster portion of the process, was having fun photographing what was about to happen. He is one of those sage old wise owls that seems to know what is going to happen long before it does.

Harlan had begun warning me about Craig months before this event, seeming to sense something in Craig's DNA, bloodstream, or demeanor that I had not picked up on. Remember, I am a rather naïve person because I don't think in deceitful terms or about how to cheat or lie to someone. It is just not in my core genetic makeup; this weakness does tend to cause me great pain at times.

But alas, the worst is over right? Wrong! We still had the rally day to get through and the best was yet to come!

I left the rally site that afternoon fairly late, just before dark as I recall, and I remember talking to Harlan on the way back to Winterset, Iowa (my hometown) and asking him, "How can people do this to other people"?

His answer was fairly simplistic, "Ken, there are still evil people in this world."

And there you have it.

ELEVEN

THE HEAVENS SAY, 'LET US COME FORTH AND RALLY'

Have you ever heard the old adage, "*It is so quiet, you can hear the corn grow?*" This is a real phenomenon. If you'd like to test its validity, find a quiet spot in the middle of a cornfield on a humid day (humidity is crucial because it plays a part in making this happen), sit down, and listen. You will hear an occasional popping noise. That is the sound of the corn growing.

The morning of September 3, 2011, was one of those days when you could hear the corn grow. During the early morning hours, the temperature was probably 80 degrees (incredibly warm for us in Central Iowa), and the sky was filled with high, puffy clouds. I couldn't shake my foreboding feeling; something just didn't feel right to me. The weather was too hot and humid, and worst of all, there wasn't a thing I could do about it.

Stopping by to pick Harlan up at the hotel, he mentioned he felt the same way as he got in my vehicle. "Ken, is it normally this hot this early in the morning?" he asked.

"No, it's not," I answered. Then he uttered the words I'd been denying since the day before.

"Do you think it is going to thunderstorm?"

I could only pray that it didn't, but it sure was beginning to look like it.

When we pulled into the gate of the facility, there were already dozens and dozens of RV's and campers parked and hooked up. These were the folks who had arrived a day ahead to visit, drink a few beers, and become acquainted with their fellow Palinistas from around the country.

I will never forget one fellow in particular, with whom I'd become quite friendly. He was such a fan of Sarah's he had legally changed his first name to Palin. Yes, really. He'd called me from Connecticut and impressed me so much I hooked him up with local radio host Simon Conway from WHO in Des Moines. Simon even interviewed him while he drove from the northeastern seaboard to Indianola for the event.

Throughout the planning process, I'd gotten to know Simon fairly well; by rally day, I'd completed four or five interviews with him about the event. A British national who became an American citizen, he is a staunch constitutionalist hired by WHO (1040 AM) as the afternoon drive-time host. The station had brought him in to replace "self-righteous religious zealot" Steve Deace, who had been fired for his on-air antics regarding the Bible and politics, which no doubt accounted for the multiple complaints from angry listeners. Simon was most assuredly going to be a hit on this Midwest blowtorch radio station: he was sharp as a tack, knew his politics, and was as quick as they come when dealing with callers on political subjects. Best of all, he'd agreed to be our emcee for our big event!

As I meandered my way around the huge parking lot greeting the many folks who had already gathered, I kept noticing that the clouds off to the north were beginning to appear ominous indeed.

I made my way across the street to the front gate and noticed that my other friend Harlan from Merhow Trailer had arrived to set up our two holding trailers. In a welcome development, he had offered to provide two gorgeous living quarters (RV types of horse trailers with air conditioning, restrooms, etc.), and trailers for the speakers and guests behind the stage. These were to be "green rooms" of sorts for the event's celebrities.

A couple of cups of coffee and a few donuts later, our VIP's had begun arriving. Since she was the headliner keynote speaker, Sarah was not due in for several more hours.

Steve Vaus arrived intact. Steve, as you may or may not know, actually won a Grammy for his music. He was scheduled to sing *We Must Take America Back*, an emotional song about how far we had sunk as a nation. I am quite fond of Steve's infectious humor, which would prove to be a life-saver for me personally on this day. As he stepped out his car with his guitar case, I noticed he was wearing a pair of custom-made cowboy boots featuring large red roses, which made me laugh out loud. He looked at me with a sheepish grin on his face and explained, "They're my lucky boots I wore at the Grammy's." Hey, who am I to laugh at success, right? My only response was, "No self-respecting cowboy in Montana would be caught dead in those boots Steve." We hugged and walked up to the holding trailers.

Krista Branch and her husband Michael arrived safe and sound as the clouds began to look even more threatening on the horizon. Krista you will recognize as the beautiful, powerful voice behind her hit song *I am America*, which became Herman Cain's campaign theme song for his White House run in 2012.

Sisters Stacie Ruth and Carrie Beth Stoelting also brought in their gorgeous patriot music laced with a Christian theme. Charlie knew them personally, for which I am grateful. They were an instant hit after they sung the National Anthem in front of the world. Subsequently, they have appeared on Fox and Friends and many other programs, singing their hymns and Christmas music.

With the arrival of Dr. Sam Clovis and his powerful patriotic messaging; fire-breathing radio voice Tony Katz; and humorous political comedian Eric Golub, we knew this was going to be an event for the history books.

As Charlie and I stood backstage surveying the beauty of the early morning and pondering our future, once again our gaze went toward the foreboding sky.

Simon Conway hit the stage precisely on time and began leading us through our ceremonial patriotic items. He introduced the minister who led us in prayer, then Charlie, who led us in the pledge, before it was onto the rousing Stoelting sisters leading us in the *Star Spangled Banner*. At that point, it was off to the races.

I hit the stage and threw some red meat (metaphorically speaking) to the crowd, as did Charlie. We offered plenty of scraps detailing the evil of Barack Obama and the utter weakness of our Congress. Of course, the crowd's enthusiastic reaction further fueled the passion in both of our orations.

At the time, one of my wife's dear friends had a son who was being treated for brain cancer at St. Jude's Hospital in Memphis, Tennessee. We brought little Bradley on stage with his parents and through my tears, I told the crowd that when Obamacare fully kicked in, this precious child's healthcare would end up being decided by the federal government. History, by the way, has proven me correct in this assessment.

With that, the heavens opened! Thousands scrambled for cover and Charlie and I looked at each other without saying a word, our facial expressions conveying the thought, "Why us? Why do we always have to be plagued with bad luck?" This was not just a normal rain shower; it turned out to be what we refer to back in Texas as a "gully-washer." Lightning struck furiously, deafening claps of thunder hurt our ears, and Mother Nature seemed to mock us by making it truly dangerous to stay in the area.

Truth be known, I have no idea what the dozens of television cameras did as I headed for one of the trailers that was at least grounded with rubber tires. The storm lasted for approximately a half-hour or so and dumped a good two inches of water, creating a muddy mess for the rest of the day. My mother, who was sitting in the front row, still hasn't forgiven me for the downpour that scared the bejeebus out of her.

As the rain finally let up and people began returning to their seats, blankets, lawn chairs, and large coolers they used for chairs, the show resumed with Eric firing up their funny bones. He did draw the ire of the mass media with one of his jokes involving Democrats and Sarah Palin's son Trig, who has Down syndrome. It was a benign joke about the Democrats' callousness toward the Governor, due to her choice to keep her son rather than abort him. To this day, I never understood why the media took the side of the Democrats but they did. Golub's joke went over with the media much like the famed German Airship Hindenburg – in other words, it didn't fly. This was strike number one for the Restoring America Rally in the tabloids.

Steve brought the crowd to their feet with his rendition of his hit song of patriotism and fighting the good fight. *We Must Take America Back* had them on their feet and singing along as Sarah's caravan arrived behind the stage. The two SUV's pulled up with her security detail, her assistants, and of course, her husband Todd, who was along for the ride.

Days before, the Sarah Palin team had all but demanded that she be introduced by a congressman, a state senator, the Governor of Iowa or anyone other than one of us. I had put my foot down and said "No." She would be introduced by either Charlie or me.

It was then that her staff relented and said "OK, but we have an introduction video" that must be played.

This was the first I had seen of this video entitled *Iowa Passion*. What I did not know was that it had been playing in the form of advertisements for the Governor. If ever there was a video that baited the public into thinking she was running for President, this was it.

A montage of clips from Sarah's bus as it traveled across Iowa and ultimately arrived at the famed Iowa State Fair, the video can still be seen on YouTube.

After Steve Vaus's hair-raising, spine-tingling version of his uber-patriotic song, the video starts with Sarah talking over film clips of her adventures in Iowa. As you can imagine, by now the crowd was in an absolute frenzy with people chanting "Sarah, Sarah, Sarah!" Even with our concert-quality sound system, one could not hear the video.

I walked across the stage to the chorus of "Sarah, Sarah, Sarah," and after the enormous brown bear had roared, I announced, "Ladies and Gentlemen, Governor Sarah Palin." She appeared from behind the curtain and gave me a warm embrace. I said, "Knock 'em dead kid," and she laughed before responding "I'll try." Then she turned to face the crowd while history and the truth began to unfold before my eyes.

You can often tell the direction a speech is going by its opening and cadence. Palin launched immediately into the red meat portion by attacking Barack Obama, crony capitalism, tyrannical behavior, and everything else that would lead one to believe it was a prelude to the words her supporters desperately wanted to hear "…and this is why I am announcing my candidacy for the Presidency of the United States of America."

After the obvious campaign video of her interacting with thousands of adoring fans at the Iowa State Fair accompanied by a voiceover which could not have been more patriotic in nature, these words never came.

Sarah Palin had just spent about 35 minutes delivering a fiery speech designed to stimulate and motivate the Patriots in the audience to take their country back – without her as their leader.

After enduring countless hours and days' worth of driving and several months of hype; after spending nearly $100,000 and losing untold amounts of sleep, this is what we got? An absolute disaster in terms of public relations for Charlie and me. Do you mean to tell me I impaled myself on a political sword for this? Why, yes! Yes, I did!

As if Sarah's disappointing speech hadn't been punishment enough (to be clear, it was a good speech, just not what we'd been led to believe it would be), the worst was yet to come for me personally.

TWELVE

STEALING A TEA PARTY 101

So you want to start a Tea Party movement but really don't want to expend the effort to do what it takes? This easy *how to* guide entitled *How to Steal a Tea Party for Dummies* (maybe that should be the actual title of this book) should teach you all you need to know.

Virtually before the Restoring America Rally had ended, the attacks began on our reputations. As I said earlier, the first launch of artillery began with press attacks against comedian Eric Golub for his joke about Sarah and her son. The next shell that burst was *"how Ken Crow had so screwed this rally up"* with the Sarah Palin and Christine O' Donnell fiasco. The last and probably the worst for Charlie and me were the cloak-and-dagger rumors that followed about *"how much money"* had been spent on this event. While there were only a few blurbs in the press about it, the real damage was being done behind the scenes.

What I was totally unaware of was the campaign Craig had started to destroy my personal reputation. I would not find out the exact nature of his actions for some three years, but in the end, I discovered the truth.

Craig had systematically approached every individual I'd thought of as a friend and laid the groundwork of me being a loose cannon, unreliable, politically inept, and any other character assassination term he could conjure up.

He engaged in this concerted effort while simultaneously befriending me and strongly suggesting that Charlie and I set up some type of permanent LLC (Limited Liability Corporation) to include a Board of Directors for Tea Party of America. Craig was correct that we needed to act fast so as to capitalize on the rally fever in order to grow the membership base.

Up until now it was generally understood, based on a handshake between Charlie and me, that we each owned 50% of Tea Party of America. We mutually agreed Craig would be an asset to the organization and that making it legitimate would attract other respected individuals as well to sit on the board. Charlie would be the Chief Executive Officer and I would be the President.

After Craig's deviously strategic placement of allies and the division of shares, we had everything in place for a working board. By now it was the middle of October and we were anxious to get started on growing Tea Party of America into the brand and organization all the other groups would want to partner with; we wanted to solidify our position as a large, behemoth monster of a political organization.

However, unknown to me, Craig was busy trashing me personally behind the scenes. This guy had a plan that was working flawlessly. Craig had teamed up with his good friend from Cedar Falls, Iowa (whom he had brought to the inner circle), his good friend April, and manipulated Charlie tirelessly, to create doubt in his mind about me.

In the end, after our first meeting of the Board of Directors at the Machine Shed Restaurant in Des Moines, Iowa, I got up from the table, said my piece, and walked away from the group. I'd made a decision to resign because the stress Craig had created simply wasn't worth it to me.

For years to come, I would stew on this decision and the events leading up to it. I was personally wounded – this had been my idea, my sweat, my tears, and my love – all for nothing. I knew it had been stolen from me as Craig had garnered enough shares by aligning himself through deceit and lies to throw me off the board and steal my organization from me anyway. And not surprisingly, I wouldn't be the only one.

Craig (and I am not exactly sure how all of this was to work) had a master plan. He had conned a pastor from Nebraska by the name of Shannon Chestnut into setting up something similar, using his dream of an organization by the name of Patriots for Christ.

Somehow, Tea Party of America was to merge with Patriots for Christ and coalesce the evangelicals with the hardcore Tea Party clan into one high-profile political power base. But Craig needed Patriots for Christ to make this happen. I have been told several different stories about the way this was supposed to work, but Craig was nearly 100% correct in his assessment that a good majority of Tea Party Nation is evangelical and it is the evangelicals in Iowa that often determine the winner of the Iowa Caucuses. Furthermore, a win in Iowa often determines a presidential candidate's ability to continue their race for the White House.

According to Shannon, the Board of Directors was put together (with many of the same folks that Craig had under his mind-game spell) and the results were exactly the same. The percentages were divided and the shaming had begun. Once again a good man's reputation was being destroyed so that Craig could garner what Craig wanted.

What Craig wanted, Craig had officially obtained – and that was control over two conservative groups that could have been extraordinarily powerful at the ballot box.

I might never know the exact truth here as to his genuine ambitions. I may never know exactly what was said about me (although I have been told quite a bit by those he talked with about me), but I do apply common sense when necessary to a situation and work myself through to the logical end.

One has to ask, "Why would this fellow want these two organizations only to shelve them?" Yes, Craig took the domain names (I sold him my rights for Tea Party of America) and basically shelved them, never to do anything with them again. Why? Why would he allow a movement to stop dead in its tracks?

Months down the road, I received a phone call late one night. Craig has many enemies, but this particular enemy is a computer geek from hell. A professional hacker, this guy is a firewall builder, or whatever you want to call him. You do not want to make enemies out of such individuals because if they choose, they can find out not just your Visa balance owed to Capitol One, but also your shoe size and blood type if they want to badly enough.

This particular guy went on to explain in the vaguest of terms that he had hacked into a bank account someplace (I honestly don't know where) and found that Craig was actually on the payroll of the Democrat Party.

Could it be that we had a spy in our midst? By this time, I had already been hearing all sorts of wild (or at least they seemed wild) stories about our friend Craig. Keep in mind that this is the guy who had started a radio show based upon conservative values, preached the Scripture, and was trying to desperately to be like his good friend Steve Deace (you remember him from earlier). Only it now appears that these efforts were nothing more than a cover to stop conservative grassroots organizing from actually happening.

I asked my friend (the geek), "*Are you sure, how do you know, can you verify this?*" and a litany of obvious questions. A problem arose when I inquired as to whether he would be willing to come forth with this proof and he unequivocally shot back, "No!" Apparently, his actions had been less than stellar, which meant he could actually get into a sizable amount of trouble for his effort, so he withdrew and said, *"I just thought you should know and I tried to tell you all along."*

Back to the "horse sense" for a moment. This would explain then how Craig had been earning a living for all those years he had been involved in Tea Party activities. Craig had no job or visible means of income. He lived in a house that his mother had bequeathed him when she passed away and he seemed to live a fairly comfortable lifestyle. So how did he live? Remember he had been a longtime political operative at one level or another, but for the past few years had not held a job for any campaign. Remember also, he knew everyone in politics.

I kept that little gem in my hip pocket for another two years or so when I was to find out (through rumor) that Craig had also stolen a tractor-trailer load of computers that belonged to Ralph Reed's organization The Christian Coalition. Remember back in the 90's when Ralph Reed teamed up with the Reverend Jerry Falwell and formed this powerful political voting bloc? Craig had worked for them back on the East Coast and as rumor has it when he left one night, the Christian Coalition was missing rooms full of computer terminals. What these terminals contained were the lists of hundreds of thousands of members which Craig could use for fundraising if he chose to do so.

It was then that I remembered Craig would periodically tell me about a trailer he owned, one he claimed was full of musical equipment. He'd lament he'd have to take tomorrow off to go sell something so that he could pay an electric bill, phone bill or some other necessity. This was during the run up to the big rally. Although I thought it odd, I honestly didn't give it too much thought since Craig always pleaded poor mouth. I usually had to pay for lunch when we worked.

Ultimately, I will never know if Craig was a paid operative of the Democrats but I can tell you with great authority, it is the only logical explanation of what happened and why it happened the way it did. Two perfectly legitimate organizations with bright futures totally destroyed and shelved. Keep in mind, both of them could've and would've made huge differences in political outcomes in the Midwest, Iowa in particular. They could have played a pivotal role in Barack Obama carrying or losing Midwestern states. These organizations could have put boots on the ground for Governor Mitt Romney, thus possibly swaying the outcome. As it stands today? Barack Obama carried Iowa and it didn't have to happen the way it did.

This would not be the end of the Craig saga, though. Karma has a funny way of leveling the playing field at times. Remember that trailer load of computers? The latest news is that the FBI knows where it is and is investigating any improprieties, and that is the latest gossip I have. If true, as the old saying goes, "Karma can be a real bitch at times."

The Tea Party of America and Patriots for Christ would not be the only patriotic organizations stolen over the years by greedy and less-than- honorable people.

Out in Sacramento, California, we have probably one the largest thefts of them all: this one involves millions of dollars and a high-profile Tea Party.

Blue Star Moms and Gold Star Moms are special people. A Blue Star Mom is the mother of a soldier, sailor, airman or Marine serving in a wartime theater overseas. A Gold Star Mom is a mother of a fallen soldier, sailor, airman or Marine, who was lost in a combat zone overseas.

Deborah Johns is a Blue Star Mom, who had watched endless days of Iraq War protesters, led by Cindy Sheehan, camped out in front of then President Bush's ranch in Crawford, Texas. She finally said *"enough is enough"* and took to the airwaves.

Johns's son, who was serving admirably in the theater, provided enough motivation for her to begin calling into various radio shows in the Sacramento and Bay Area in defense of these gallant soldiers. Where Sheehan was bashing our activities in Iraq, Johns was telling the stories coming back, via her son, of how our brave soldiers were helping Iraqi citizens and how the average Iraqi loved our honorable men and women in uniform.

The main target of Deborah Johns recitations was Sacramento's news station KFBK and the Mark Williams show. After months of reverse protesting and telling heartwarming stories, Deborah had obviously become a known entity who was quite adept at radio appearances. By now a radio superstar named Jim Bohannon had heard her often enough, he began contacting her for interviews. The nationally syndicated talk show host began interviewing Johns on his show.

After months and months of interviews, another prominent radio figure heard Deborah Johns passion and decided to contact her. Keep in mind, this is around the time Arizona Senator John McCain was doing well in the primaries and it looked as though he was most likely going to win the nomination back in 2008.

Johns was contacted by a fellow by the name of Sal Russo , who owned King Media. As Deborah tells the story, Sal was in partnership with a fellow by the name of Howard Kaloogian. Both Sal and Howard were long-time Republican operatives from California. According to Wikipedia, Sal and Howard operated a political consulting firm that also owned a Political Action Committee named *Our Country Deserves Better* PAC. It would be this PAC that Sal and Howard would use to form Tea Party Express.

The two had decided they wanted Deborah Johns to be the "front-person and spokesperson" for the new Tea Party, which was formed in the summer of 2009.

Politics is a small world in many ways. The word was already on the street that Tea Party Patriots had been formed by Jenny Beth Martin, a house cleaner from Georgia; Amy Kremer, a flight attendant for Delta Airlines; and Mark Meckler, an Attorney from California.

These two very prominent Tea Party organizations forming on the heels of the now infamous Santelli Rant were about to explode in prominence and popularity. With the explosions came enormous amounts of cash and with the cash came the snakes.

THIRTEEN

THE KINGDOM AND THE POWER

The problem with being the ruler of your own private little kingdom is that everyone beneath you wants your job title. If you're King, then all your subjects want you to go away so one of them can assume your title.

The President of the United States, for instance, has 535 other folks surrounding him who also want to be president, and this number doesn't even include cabinet officials or the 50 state governors who desire the office. Power is the ultimate aphrodisiac I am told; those who have it want to keep it and those who don't want to acquire it.

By 2012, the Tea Party had grown in excess of 600 separate organizations across America, not including the 9/12 groups (remember, these were inspired by Glenn Beck). Additionally, many new 2nd Amendment coalitions and other grassroots groups were springing up everywhere.

All of this amounted to 600 separate little political kingdoms, each with a ruler who more often than not, ruled with an iron fist.

As I wax philosophically about power, you're probably wondering why I am wandering down this path. By their example, Jenny Beth

Martin, Amy Kremer, and the rest of the Tea Party leaders would give many others the motivation and desire to attain the same status. Martin, Kremer, Meckler, Phillips, et al., had figured out a way to score large sums of cash while masking and wrapping it all up in the banner of 'patriotism' with the mantra of "We are saving the nation from the evil Barack Obama and his regime."

After over three years of receiving fundraising emails from the Tea Party Patriots, everyone in the Tea Party movement had figured out, *"Hey this is a potentially lucrative business."* I can stand on stage and be important for a little while, possibly become famous, and make money, all while saving America? This is a pretty good gig. Naturally, it was the aphrodisiac of money and fame which drove Patriots to turn on each other and eat their young.

The lure of being stalked by reporters, doing interviews, advertising their websites, and receiving large donations all in the name of conservative patriotism seduced many into doing things they normally would have never done.

The friendship of Amy Kremer and Jenny Beth would not last. While the details of their breakup are somewhere above the *Top Secret* level, it is widely speculated that the two became embroiled in a "power-grab" situation, resulting in Amy's ouster from Tea Party Patriots.

It was rumored that upon leaving, Amy had taken the *LIST* with her. According to the rumor mill, this list is the lifeblood of any 501 (c) (3) organization, for it contains the donor pool. Apparently, it provided the foundation for the ongoing lawsuits between Amy and Jenny that dragged on for years.

Basically, here's how it goes down: you land on the Patriots website for whatever reason. You decide you want to join and enter all of your information, which then goes into a database. This includes basic information about yourself and depending on the site (all sites are different), your political affiliation, mailing address, email address, willingness to volunteer, and a few more questions. In reality, the cold hard truth is that the only thing they truly care about is your email address.

Here is an example: if I own 1,000,000 email addresses (which I know are verified and good), I can earn literally millions of dollars annually with this list.

Assuming my message is compelling, here is what happens. Barack Obama makes a speech about guns. I know my group is comprised of hard-core patriots who love their guns and the 2nd Amendment. Let's say this speech is on a Tuesday night after a mass shooting (this really did happen by the way). By Wednesday at noon, you will have an email in your inbox that stating that Obama is making a major gun grab and you're about to lose your guns.

The message will usually be about four paragraphs in length and implore you to donate now to the Tea Party Patriots because we're fighting for your gun rights and will protect them from Obama's evil clutches. As the only ones who can save your guns, the Patriots need your money to fight Barack Obama.

With that sort of message on the heels of Obama's speech, you can bet at least 3-5% of the recipients will respond (at least they did in the early days). So now we have some 50,000 panic-stricken Patriots sending in $20-25 each to save their guns from Barack Obama. Do this once a week and what happens? Keep in mind that is just 1,000,000 emails; Jenny Beth had touted on several occasions that the Patriots had some 15,000,000 members.

There was a point in time between 2009 and 2011-2012 (leading up to the general elections) where I personally would receive three or four of these compelling emails weekly. Do the math! Averages say that if you send out some 45,000,000 emails weekly with only a 1% return, that is 450,000 donors giving at the rate of $20 average – so what do we have?

Now you can understand why Jenny Beth was so eager to seize control of the Tea Party Patriots, "lock, stock, and barrel." The revenue streams into the organization were simply mind-blowing. Of course, it would not be for several more years that the Patriots would form an actual Political Action Committee to support or attack candidates in a more direct way (which only PAC's can legally do). Up until then, for some five or more years, Tea Party Patriots had virtually no accountability with respect to their fundraising actions. Jenny Beth Martin was literally in charge and she owned this money-making machine.

It was just a matter of time before Meckler (the brains behind the fundraising to begin with) would be on the streets looking for a job. Again, this too is top-secret since everyone was paid off to remain quiet about the inner-workings of the Patriots.

At the time of Amy's departure, nobody had any idea what she was like as a personality. Deborah Johns reached out to her for the purpose of welcoming her into the Tea Party Express, expecting (as most of the Tea Party folks do) true patriotism, love for our nation, and a fighting spirit to take on the liberalism invading our hallowed halls of Washington, D. C..

When you talk with Deborah about bringing Kremer into the fold, she often becomes depressed and sentimental – just as I do when discussing the circumstances that caused me to walk away from the Tea Party of America. You pour your heart and soul into something honorable as Johns and I did respectively, only to have it snatched away by less than scrupulous people.

Deborah Johns brought Amy Kremer into the fold only to have Amy thank her by stirring up rumors, going behind her back, and undermining her credibility, just as Craig had done with me. Economically speaking, you can now see why Kremer was so eager to rid the Express of Johns. Johns was in the movement for the right reasons while Kremer was in it for vastly different ones (apparently, pure speculation on my part). Johns was the outspoken pretty face who was getting all the press time and Kremer wasn't.

I will say this much on behalf of the Tea Party Express: Sal Russo and his partners at their SuperPAC, at least, had the decency to put much of what they were raising back into elections (according to the website Open Secrets). I cannot say the same for the Tea Party Patriots.

As you will note by these screen capture shots from Open Secrets.org, the Tea Party Express Citizens Funds PAC raised some $14,000,000 and change in the election cycle of 2014. (As a side note, I honestly wish I had kept the hundreds of fundraising emails I received in that midterm cycle from these guys. You would be amazed at some of their reasoning for needing money).

I received emails telling me that if I donated today, the Patriots were going to replace John Boehner as Speaker of the House, accompanied by a litany of reasons why he was a bad speaker. Others informed me that the Patriots were fighting for the Keystone Pipeline and my gasoline prices would drop if I donated. Still others announced they were going to force Obama to drop his fight against coal and therefore, my heating rates would not increase. Yes, a little of that is tongue in cheek, but you get the idea. The Tea Party Patriots' Citizen's Fund was truly utilizing (former Obama Chief of Staff) Rahm Emanuel's mantra of *"don't ever let a good crisis go to waste."* Whatever crisis they could come up with in the headlines on any particular day they used to solicit money from hard-working, freedom-loving patriots across the fruited plain (as Rush Limbaugh likes to say).

With some $14-plus million in donations, the Patriots are now ready to do battle on Capitol Hill, right? Let's look closer. Keep in mind, these are the numbers the Citizens Fund turned over to the Federal Election Commission.

With nearly $15,000,000 in donations, they actually spent $0 on candidates in terms of donations. What? No money spent on candidates at all? *Nope*, would be the answer. How about advertising for or against candidates? Here they did a little better, investing $1,400,000 in campaigns of some sort.

This leaves the $64,000 question: where did some $13,000,000 go? According to the filings, it went toward expenses. Expenses for what?

My point here is to be careful where you send your money. For this Political Action Committee/Tea Party to be raking in the sorts of numbers you're reading about and get so little done regarding actual movement in Washington makes one wonder, *what are they doing with all that money?*

I have attended rallies in Washington. I have spoken on the steps of the United States Capital. I have been involved with organizing events in many states as well as our nation's capital. You can hold an enormous rally in D.C. for a reasonable amount of money. You can set it up on the cheap for just tens of thousands or you can do a full-scale blow-out for one-hundred or two-hundred thousand. In either case, you will not spend $13 million dollars holding rallies to protest a health care bill. So again, I ask, who has the money?

This scenario repeated itself dozens upon dozens upon more dozens of times across our land. Smaller groups would form with the best of intentions, a few would get it in their head that they could do a better job and raise more money, then they would seize power by destroying the original founder's reputation.

The infighting amongst the smaller groups was only surpassed by the infighting of the larger ones. The entire purpose of the Tea Party of America was to bring all these groups under one banner with competent leadership, the proper political strategist, and the right counsel, in order to do a professional job in Washington. Had the groups been willing to work toward one goal, we could have actually become a force that no elected official would have been willing to tangle with.

Alas, others don't see it that way. Time and time again, I would call a group or speak with a group, only to be told that the power of the Tea Party is its "individualism." We can all see how well that has worked out, can't we?

FOURTEEN

HERDING CATS WOULD BE EASIER

I recently wrote this article upon learning that Speaker of the House Paul Ryan had agreed to sign on to the $1.2 Trillion dollar Omnibus bill.

Hey Tea Party, Time to Declare WAR on Speaker Paul Ryan

Time and again the Tea Parties in the Badger State have flexed their political muscle and time and again they have prevailed. The Tea Party groups in Wisconsin have proven in the past three election cycles, they are tough, they are organized and they will work hard to protect or support the candidate of their respective choice. This was particularly true of the support they gave Wisconsin Governor Scott Walker when he was so viciously attacked by labor union-backed Democrats for a recall election.

In the closely contested elections financed and backed by big labor, the grassroots hard work of Wisconsin's Tea Party and conservative groups prevailed to keep a conservative at the helm of the great State of Wisconsin.

Last October, America's Tea Party and Conservative movement made a decision to trust Congressman Paul Ryan with the most powerful position in the House of Representatives, that being the coveted position of Speaker of the House. Ryan promised to adhere to conservative values and govern from a perspective of smaller government, less spending, and lower taxes. American security would be paramount for his agenda.

As all of you have heard, Speaker Ryan did not just break his pledge to conservatism, he baptized his role as Speaker with nothing short of liberal holy water.

I won't rehash what all is in this behemoth $1.2 Trillion dollar spending monstrosity, but for conversation purposes, just know that it funds everything that slaps conservatism in the face and spits on Tea Party values. Breitbart wrote a great article that you can read here to get the full low-down on just how bad this darned thing is. If Obama's spending wasn't bad enough, this Omnibus spending bill also funds those cities which harbor illegal aliens and much, much more that is sure to hack off those of us that love our nation.

If this Omnibus bill is any sort of indication of the way Speaker Ryan is going to govern, it is time to do what "***Barney Fife***" told us to do so many years ago, "**NIP-IT, NIP-IT**" in the bud now!

All patriots should contact your groups' leaders and begin organizing nationwide to put down this RINO so that he is not re-elected to his seat in Wisconsin. The Badger State Patriots need to begin soliciting your state senators, high-profile business leaders or the state legislators who reside within the 1st District of Wisconsin.

Apparently nobody in the 1st District has announced any intention of forcing Ryan into a primary, but it is time to locate someone willing to do this who might actually have a chance (with enough grassroots support) at defeating our newest RINO-Speaker. America doesn't need another John Boehner but that is apparently what we now have as Speaker of the House.

<u>This is the part that is critical patriots!</u>

If the local Wisconsin Tea Party groups can locate a candidate willing to primary Paul Ryan in the 1st District, this candidate will need a truckload of cash to make it an actual race. That candidate will need our full support. This means we all need to reach deep and find an extra $10 or $20.00 bill to send to this candidate. If 200 or 300,000 of us do this, now we have a very real chance of knocking off Ryan in the primary and winning the general election. Currently, Paul Ryan has around $5,000,000 in his campaign coffers.

Patriots, get on the phones, start calling the Wisconsin groups and get them in gear to find us a candidate. After this has been accomplished, have a very Merry Christmas and a safe and Happy New Year, then it's time to get to work!

Wisconsin Patriots, LET me know what you need and we at Crows Nest will post it for everyone to rally to your aid.

We cannot allow these politicians to stand and lie to us in this matter. Paul Ryan has broken every promise he made and for that, he must pay the political price.

This article was actually picked up by Fox News, CNN and most major political publications across America. Why would the major media grab this article and basically promote it?

The first answer that comes to mind is, *"Hey the GOP is turning on itself."* As a website owner, I can't say I was complaining much. The article picked up some 12,000 LIKES in the first 48 hours of publication and any site owner in their right mind is going to like that sort of thing. But what happened next was very puzzling to me.

My friend James Murphy, President of the Green Bay Tea Party contacted me. He was all-in for trying to dump Paul Ryan.

I do need to give you some back story here on why a Tea Party would be anti-Speaker Ryan in the first place. Most people hold an illusion of Paul Ryan as a super conservative, fiscal bean-counting wonk, for a lack of better description. This label was applied to him when he was being sold as Governor Mitt Romney's running mate in the 2012 general election. The establishment had thought they could sell him to the Tea Party as a fiscally conservative wonk. (Their words not mine),

What had apparently happened was that Drudge or some other prominent blogger picked up my article because "I was calling for the ouster" of Paul Ryan. Indeed, I was. My post immediately made national political news and I began receiving phone calls.

James asked if I could help and almost immediately, I said yes. "What do you need from me? I will help any way I can," was my first and only response to James Murphy, who inquired if I could help raise money for this effort. Unbeknownst, there was significant infighting among the Wisconsin Tea Party organizations.

The next day, I received a call from a woman in Southern California on the heels of Murph's call. This professional lady explained that the Tea Parties in Wisconsin are split pretty evenly between being ultra conservative to supporting Paul Ryan; those groups are considered to be moderate. The reason she knows this, in spite of living in Southern

California, is because before relocating to The Golden State, she was a leader in Wisconsin who knows all the players personally.

Hey look, I had a simple request here. All I wanted was for the groups to get together as you had done back when Mark Block was such a player in Wisconsin, toss Ryan out on his head, and get a more conservative speaker like Marsha Blackburn from Tennessee. Is that too much to ask?

"Yep!" That's all she said. "Yep!"

Here's the report on Paul Ryan in Washington: he is extremely popular and the fact is, the position of Speaker of the House is extraordinarily powerful if you're a member of the House of Representatives. The position of Speaker controls the appointments to committees and basically determines your political future if you're a Congressman. In other words, if you have committee assignments (such as Agriculture, Appropriations, Armed Services, Budget, etc.) then you can go back to North Dakota and campaign on the fact that "your position on the Agriculture Committee" is what brought back this $60,000,000.00 in pork last session for your state. This is what makes these folks so very tough to get rid of, once they win their seat in Washington.

If you are on the Armed Services Committee and you save the Air Force Base in Montana, you are pretty much guaranteed a seat in Washington until you die or want to retire to fly fish for the rest of your days.

The bottom line is, the only way to get these seats and a guaranteed job (for life) with unlimited funding from the 'National Republican Congressional Committee' (for reelection), is by kissing up to the Speaker (as he is the one that hands them out) and not rocking the boat so to speak.

With all this said, *"How do we get rid of Speaker Paul Ryan?"*

The only practical way to do it is to 'unseat' him in his own district. Remember, it was Kevin McCarthy (Republican-California) who was to be the heir apparent to the long-serving John Boehner (Republican-Ohio).

Rifling back through your memory banks, remember when I talked about that huge party swing back in 2010 earlier in the book. Part of that massive swing were 42 uber-conservative types. While this number doesn't seem like a lot, it actually is. Without those 42, the Republicans don't have enough votes to secure the Speaker they want. With the 42, they do. The gang of 42 isn't enough to get it done on their own, but it is enough to stop the elites from getting another Boehner or heir to Boehner's thrown.

This is why McCarthy lost when he was supposed to be the one to secure the seat. It was articles in Politico, The Hill, Crows Nest Politics and countless others that caused a flurry of phone calls to House members by upset Tea Party folks who did not want the moderate McCarthy to be the next speaker.

With the decision now made as to *"How we get rid of Ryan"* (the negotiated successor to Boehner), it was time to start mobilizing the Tea Party in Wisconsin.

Since I knew Murphy, I figured he was a natural to collaborate with on *"who we could get to run and primary Paul Ryan."* What I did not anticipate was the visceral reaction I would get from so many on differing sides of the fence. Not me personally, but I would learn of the warring factions within the Wisconsin Tea Party movement.

Paul Ryan serves in Wisconsin's 1st District which is Milwaukee, Janesville and that southern area just north of the Illinois border. Apparently, Tea Parties in that area of Wisconsin are on the somewhat more moderate side of the aisle in terms of their love for Ryan.

On the one hand, I had the hard-charging Murphy (a Patrick Henry clone) who dislikes moderates and would just as soon feed them to wolves. And on the other hand, I was getting phone calls from moderate Tea Party folks telling me that Murphy was a nut-job who needed a padded cell.

At this point, I pretty much decided that maybe this effort truly wasn't worth it. I mean how bad is Paul Ryan? If you're a hard-charging Tea Party person, he is the devil incarnate. If you are a middle of the road sort of conservative, he is widely hailed as "right up your ally" regarding political affiliation.

This episode of short-lived affiliation and self-induced body-bashing I took in Wisconsin further solidified my thoughts as to just how dysfunctional Americas Tea Parties truly are. Wisconsin is hardly the only example of the Tea Party's misuse of their significant power and their inability to utilize their full potential. Most Tea Party groups fall short in this regard.

Iowa probably remains the best example of Tea Party dysfunctionality in America today. The state is full of Tea Parties, most of which are active in local Iowa politics. We have an organization here named *Iowa Grassroots Coalition,* which meets quarterly. This organization is a blueprint for what actually needs to happen across America.

It includes 9/12 groups, 2nd Amendment groups, Constitutional advocacy groups, Tea Party groups, politically charged Christian groups, anti-common core educational groups, pro-life, and pro-traditional marriage groups, and many more. Altogether there are around 50 or so grassroots "Tea Partyish" groups that umbrella under the Iowa Grassroots Coalition.

One of the leaders of this organization is a lady from Northwest Iowa by the name of Tammy Kobza. A hardworking patriot and as nice of a person as you'll ever meet, Tammy will be the first to admit that "to get all these folks on the same page" is like trying to *herd cats*!

FIFTEEN

MEET MY FRIEND BINKY

A couple of years ago, during the 2014 midterm election cycle, a friend called to ask what I was doing in March. At that time, it was still cold and snowy in Iowa. This particular friend inquired as to what I thought about possibly trekking my way to Sioux Falls, South Dakota to work on a Republican Senate campaign.

After visiting with the candidate, Jason Ravnsborg (oh, heck, you could have just Googled this, so I might as well tell you) on the phone, we agreed that I would go up and meet with him. I found him to be tremendously passionate and committed in his beliefs across a wide range of topics. A Christian and an attorney in the Southeastern part of the state, Jason (last name is pronounced Roundsburg) comes from the all-American family (his parents are farmers in Iowa), loves guns, and served in Iraq, for which he was awarded the Bronze Star. In other words, if I wanted to mail-order a candidate for public office, I couldn't have selected one with better credentials than Jason Ravnsborg.

Highly energized and motivated, he had already been working his tail off for his campaign. He told me (and I believe him) he had been "gripping and grinning" his way across most of the eastern part of South Dakota, which is known as East River.

Politically speaking, South Dakota is a bit strange in many ways. The state is separated into eastern and western portions by the Missouri River, which runs almost dead center north and south. East River leans heavily Democrat in its largest city, Sioux Falls. If memory serves correctly, Democrat voters outnumber Republican voters by 60-40.

Sioux Falls is fairly progressive in the sense that it is home to some high-tech industries including software companies, insurance companies and so on. Much of the city is newer and spotlessly clean, with no pollution, perpetually bright blue skies, and a warm, friendly population. Yeah, I would be happy to spend my remaining days in or around Sioux Falls; nice place!

West River (the western part of the state) is still the wild, wild west. Years ago, in the early 90's, I spent some time in the western end of South Dakota. Call this an attention deficit moment, but I think the story I'm about to share is worth telling to give you a clear idea of what I mean.

As you may or may not know, I used to be deeply involved in the rodeo arena. After years spent riding bulls, I went to the other end of the spectrum and began roping. I invested 20 years of life, first as a youth, then as an adult, in the rodeo. Some days, I performed decently and on others… well, let's just say you might have thought I had just fallen out of bed and tried to ride something.

The reason for the back story?

When I got to South Dakota, I, of course, had limited funds which made getting a job a necessity. Since I had worked in sales in the car business for many years, it was easy for me to find work as a salesperson and I landed a position at the Ford dealership in Spearfish.

My "home away from home" became a small mom and pop

motel down the road in Sturgis (home to the largest motorcycle rally on the planet, as every Harley Davidson owner knows). The motel sat right next door to a small truck stop which had a great café where I retrieved my morning breakfast. Lunch took place in Spearfish while I typically ate my supper in Deadwood.

Being from a ranch in Texas and still wearing my Wranglers daily, I, of course, fell passionately in love with the Blackhills of South Dakota and all it had to offer. The people are incredible – their smiling faces and great senses of humor, coupled with their endless supply of wild tales made me feel right at home. There is nearly zero crime of any kind and they seem to welcome newcomers with open arms.

At the time, I was in my early 30's and loving life in general; I felt like I had died and gone to a cowboy version of Mecca. Wide open spaces, good money from my job at the dealership, great food, and I could learn how to play poker at night in Deadwood – something I engaged in 5-6 times per week. Deadwood had just recently legalized low-limit gaming and the little town was exploding just as it had done back in the gold rush days in the late 1870's.

Saloon #10 was one of the top spots to drink, dance, and play cards if you could handle the rowdy nature of the place. I quickly learned that it was the old #10 where Wild Bill Hickock had met his demise by being shot in the back of the head by the drifter named Jack McCall. Yes, you too can this very day, go to Saloon #10, order a beer, sit, and play poker in the very same corner that none other than Wild Bill himself was shot and killed in. If you would like to pay your respects to Wild Bill, he is buried on top of the hill in the cemetery next to Calamity Jane overlooking Deadwood. I'll save that history lesson for another book, but the two of them had an intriguing love affair.

Throughout my adventures in Deadwood, I came across an interesting fellow by the name of Binky Steele. Don't laugh, that was his actual name. Binky passed away a number of years ago, but when

I met him, he was actually one of the Chiefs of the Sioux Nation at Pine Ridge, although I'm not certain how high of a level he'd achieved. His actual birth name was Cheyenne Yellowbird. In fact, there used to be a grocery store/gas station in Pine Ridge named *Yellowbirds*, which was his family business.

My first interaction with Binky took place when he came into the dealership one day to look at a pickup truck. He noticed I was wearing one of my trophy buckles and inquired about the events I'd participated in, wanting to know how high I had risen in the rodeo world. After I had obliged, he responded, "Great, want to judge a bull-riding event I'm holding next week?" Foolishly I answered, "No problem, happy to help."

It turned out that Binky owned a string of bulls and was getting into the latest version of rodeo for fans by holding *Bull Manias*. I equate a Bull Mania with Nascar; fans attend NASCAR races more for the crashes than the races themselves. For whatever reason, people love to watch a good crash. They don't want to see anyone get hurt, but they do love watching #25 fly through the air and then go end-over-end through the midfield. A Bull Mania is identical: it has all the excitement with crashes and cowboys flying through space. Even better, you don't have to sit and watch girls chasing stationary cans. The first event is bull riding, the second event is bull riding, and the last event is bull riding. Naturally this was beginning to take off, with great success.

As I pulled my truck onto the rodeo grounds on top of a little hill in some of the most beautiful country in America, the wind was blowing the knee-high prairie grass gently in the wind. The clouds were high and puffy and in some areas there were still buffalo grazing on the high plains.

Since the start of the performance was several hours away, Binky and I sat on the back tailgate of my pickup truck drinking Coke while the bulls stomped their feet and bellowed in the background.

After I had asked several questions, Binky indulged me by sharing his heritage. His great-grandmother was named "Cheyenne Woman." Decades before, someone had written a book about her. If my memory is accurate, Binky was in his mid- to- late 60's when we had this conversation. Cheyenne Woman had given birth to a child who had been adopted by an attorney from Oklahoma back in the 1880's. The child moved to Oklahoma but came back to the reservation as an adult.

Somewhere in his 50's, he had fathered a son who again fathered several children when he was in his 50's and 60's. As Binky was telling me this story, his head hung low; I could visibly tell there was not once ounce of pride in this saga.

"So what was the problem Binky? Why are you so sad?" I asked.

He then boldly stated that the child who went to Oklahoma and became his grandfather was none other than the child of General George Armstrong, otherwise known as Custer!

"You mean to tell me that your grandfather was Custer?" I gasped.

"Yep!"

Apparently, Native Americans take this sort of thing seriously. Poor Binky had lived with this family history his entire life and wore it as a badge of shame rather than honor. I actually felt sorry for him. But the fact was, I was drinking a Coke with the grandson of one of the most infamous Wild West characters in American history. To validate this story, I actually did a bit of research and the timeline worked out: Custer had died in 1876 up the road at Little Big Horn. He had spent an enormous amount of time in the Black Hills region and it was his expeditionary party several years before that had actually discovered gold in the hills, a phenomenon that started the great migration west in the first place.

In the Indian folklore, it was widely known that Custer had a Sioux concubine of sorts and had fathered an illegitimate child. This is why at Little Big Horn, the women actually protected his body. The rest of the soldiers were carved up and had their genitals cut off and stuffed into their mouths (the Indians believed you could not face your God if you had your privates hanging out of your mouth). Custer was simply shot and killed, then buried before he was later moved back east and given a military honors funeral.

My experience with Binky was not to end as peacefully as it had begun at the car dealership and continued during the hour we'd spent talking and drinking Coke on the back of my pickup truck. Fans and cowboys began pouring into the rodeo grounds for the *All-Indian Bull Mania* and you could feel the electricity in the air. By the time the performance started, we had probably 2,000-2,500 folks in the arena. While many of them sat in the stands, there were many others who'd pulled their trucks up the fence and sat in lawn chairs in the back. Ah yes, this was nostalgic for me personally as this was the way we did it back in the good old days in Texas.

The first cowboy to hit the arena on his bull did a marvelous job and stayed inside the arena. I say this tongue-in-cheek because before the evening was over, a couple of fellows actually landed in the gravel *outside* of the arena. Other than bumps, bruises, torn shirts, and wounded pride, they all survived Binky's bruising string of bulls.

Then came *American Spotted Pony*! Keep in mind, I am a "gringo" sort of fellow, meaning I am not Native American, nor was I accustomed to names like Soaring Eagle or American Spotted Pony. Pony was a handsome little fellow; he had a fan club I was about to meet, parked about ten feet away in a green Ford pickup truck.

Spotted Pony's fan club consisted of about eight young ladies, all in the age range of approximately 18-22. They sat in lawn chairs screaming out his name; you would have thought Elvis had reincarnated as a bull-riding cowboy.

In bull-riding, there are a couple of rules.

primarily due to Jason getting in the race late and calling me even later. Had I known what was coming, I would have been up visiting with these groups months earlier and brought them into the fold for my candidate.

3. Dr. Annette Bosworth: The good doctor had some issues in this election, the first of which being her husband. She is married to a fellow who apparently has multiple skeletons in his closet from business deals out in Utah. I never did get the exact lowdown on the specifics so I will refrain from mentioning them, but political gossip across South Dakota was that both he and Annette were pretty much sent packing from *The Beehive State* back home to South Dakota. These rumors persisted throughout this campaign cycle and were no doubt taking a toll on her success. However, she was more of a problem than he was. It seemed that the good doctor got into some trouble over her petition sheets. Apparently what had happened was that her staff went around asking potential voters to sign the necessary petitions to get her on the ballot early – as all the candidates are required to do.

However, here's where the problem arises. As she does annually, the Dr. Bosworth had gone overseas to do some volunteer work. When she returned, her staff presented her with stacks of signed petition sheets. But the candidate is required to sign a sheet stating that they had witnessed these signatures *as voters were signing them*. Even though she'd been in the Philippines at the time of their signing, she signed the sheets on those dates, as if she'd been there to see it. *Oops*, this incident would raise its ugly head later on and become a major lightening rod in this campaign. Other than a small felony (err, 20-something felonies as each signature is regarded as a felony), she was bright, vivacious and a lovely candidate. A mother to an all-American family, I never saw her when she wasn't smiling. Dr. Annette was somewhat quirky and reminded me of an eclectic Cyndi Lauper (the singer who bought her clothes at Goodwill) with a stethoscope.

Politically speaking, her positions tended to lean liberal. She is a doctor who runs a charity (or income-based) medical clinic in Sioux Falls and loves people. While she claims to be a conservative Republican, her messaging and positions are in somewhat disagreement.

4. Larry Rhoden: South Dakota State Senator (Majority Whip) Larry is the poster child for a South Dakota rancher. He nearly always wears his cowboy boots even when wearing a suit and tie. He always drives his pickup truck, has large calloused hands from years of hard work, and a warm personality. His rancher's wife, also the epitome of warmth, was constantly by his side. This gracious couple is devoted to the Great State of South Dakota. Larry (God love his heart) will never match Mike Rounds in terms of being a smooth-talking politician. If anything, as lovable as he is, he has more of a personality that resembles the character from Winnie-The-Pooh series, *Eeyore*. While likable, he is one of those fellows who seems to be perpetually "low-energy" and never gets excited about anything. His monotone speeches literally put audiences to sleep. When one is campaigning, it's critical to inspire one's listeners – not give them tryptophan and send them off to dreamland. Otherwise, Larry is good people and someone you would be honored to call a friend.

I was to stay at the Marriot in Sioux Falls for the duration of the campaign. The hotel was in a very nice part of town, the kind that was more of a business venue than an actual hotel. Every room was a suite rather than an actual room. The campaign would be renting my room by the month rather than by the night and I enjoyed amenities like a a gym, pool and full breakfast every morning. I had my WiFi as well as plugins, so I could actually hardwire my computer rather than live on the WiFi. As I walked into my room the first day, I began thinking, *"hey, I could get used to this."*

It was late afternoon when I arrived and hunger had taken hold of me. As I headed across the street to the trusty *HyVee* grocery story (all HyVee's have a wonderful buffet, Chinese Food and homemade pizza cooked in a brick oven), I stopped and visited with a young lady for a few moments at the convenience store on the way as I filled up my vehicle. I always ask young people, *"who do you like in this race?"*

She had not a clue!

For some reason, this sort of incensed me and I inquired as to "why" she had not a clue. She promptly informed me that while *she was old enough to vote, she just never paid any attention to politics because it was boring, all the politicians lied and her vote would not count anyway.*

It was at that moment that I decided to go "full-on Tea Party" and verbally spank her. I asked her if she had ever been to a National Cemetery. She asked what it was.

"Oh my God, I thought!"

I began explaining that America had set up national cemeteries across our nation and we even had them overseas to bury our fallen who had died in a war or had served our nation. I then began describing Arlington National Cemetery (where my father is buried) and the over 440,000 soldiers, sailors, airman, and marines who are buried there. She then asked, *"why are you telling me this?"*

My response was pretty simple and to the point.

"Hun, those men, and women are lying at those national cemeteries because they paid the ultimate price in order that you could vote! This is one of the few countries on earth where your vote does count and voting is what preserves liberty and freedom. Those men died so you could be free. The next time you go by a national cemetery, you stop and walk across those grounds and tell all those white crosses that their sacrifice didn't

matter because you don't have time to vote or care because you don't like politics."

By this point, she was reaching for the tissues and I was ready to start campaigning! As I left the store, she was swearing to me she would vote and get involved. Mission Accomplished!

The next morning at 8:00 AM, I meandered down to the café where the hotel was serving breakfast for my first meeting with Jason since my arrival. As we ate, he began briefing me on the status of his campaign and all the players. Jason had ZERO staff and Mike Rounds had a complete staff with millions in his campaign coffers. These millions had apparently been picked up from making numerous trips back to Washington and visiting with all the Super-PACs and lobbyists. Rounds had a complete fundraising team and even had a debate and speech coach to make sure that he was able to nuke the competition when the debates came.

It was at this meeting that I also learned of our possible pathway to victory. In South Dakota if no candidate surpasses 35% of the vote in the primaries, then the top two candidates go to a run-off election to determine who the nominee is to run against the Democrat in the November general election.

With Rounds controlling the middle and more moderate factions of the Republican Party, and Stace Nelson being the Tea Party favorite, where was Ravnsborg supposed to glean votes?

"From both ends," I was informed.

It seems that *Smiling Mike* (as he is known in South Dakota) did have a dark past or, at least, part of it was dark. He even had a dead body lying around, or rather, hanging around his neck.

"Huh, say what?" was my shell-shocked response.

What follows below is actually the best explanation of this scandal-ridden tale in which I became involved. I lifted it from Wikipedia as I could not come up with a better way to describe it.

Rounds was widely seen as the front-runner throughout the campaign. However, he faced ongoing criticism on the election trial for his possible involvement with the State's ongoing EB-5 Visa investigation concerning the conflict of interest that Rounds' administration had when administering the EB-5 program. State officials misused funds to pay for their salaries, did not disclose that they owned companies which they gave contracts to, directed money towards companies that went bankrupt and arranged for loans from unknown sources from shell companies located in tax havens. In October 2014, Rounds admitted that he had approved a $1 million state loan to meat-packing company Northern Beef shortly after learning that Secretary of Tourism and State Development Richard Benda had agreed to join the company with Benda then getting another $600,000 in loans that were ultimately used to pay his own salary. Benda committed suicide in October 2013, days before a possible indictment over embezzlement and grand theft charges.

A couple of key points need to be made here. To this day, even in Presidential campaigns, you will hear candidates talk about these EB-5 Visa programs. The program was set up to allow foreign workers to come in and work, the hiring company to receive tax breaks, and Americans to lose jobs. That is the bottom line, but the silver lining for the company owners is they get cheaper labor and a fatter bottom line profit margin. Yes, this is one of the reasons the Tea Party is so infuriated with the moderates who set this up to benefit their big donors who own the companies that hire these EB-5 Visa workers in the first place.

After listening to this sordid tale of corruption, misappropriation of funds (all going back to Smiling Mike), illegal immigrants coming in for cheap labor, Cyndi Lauper (posing as a doctor), Eeyore, and an Angry Marine as competition, I began to see a pathway to victory after all. I thought, "Hey, I can force a run-off election here," then pound Smiling Mike with this EB-5 Visa fiasco and we might just pull this off.

After further questioning of my candidate Jason, I learned that this scandal was actually a very big deal in South Dakota. He went on to explain that South Dakota residents are very cognizant of where their tax revenues are spent, who is spending them, and why. In other words, these folks are plugged into their state's governmental system pretty closely.

The bottom line was, if I could figure out a way to heighten the visibility of this scandal and wrap it around Rounds neck, we could dilute his popularity significantly with the voters of South Dakota.

As a candidate, Jason was far and away more polished than any of the other candidates other than Smiling Mike himself. Our fair-haired doctor Cyndi wore almost the same clothes that the singer did while on the campaign trail with the personality to match her wardrobe. Eeyore was tragically boring and created almost zero excitement, while Stace repeated the same old, "I'm just a Marine who loves my country speech."

The one twist to this saga was that Cyndi "Annette Bosworth" Lauper had been raising a boatload of money, which was making Smiling Mike nervous. As it turned out, Bosworth's husband was somewhat of a social media guru and had been attracting thousands upon thousands of followers on Facebook who were all donating $15-20 at a pop. Thus, she'd legitimately raised over a $1,000,000 in her own right. This made Smiling Mike very, very nervous because this young lady was actually becoming quite popular.

Rounds had apparently figured out that if she could penetrate his popularity with spending some fairly serious money and Nelson could grab the conservative vote, this would force Smiling Mike below that 35% threshold and he would have to campaign again in a heads-up match. He didn't want this outcome because he'd run the risk of having to answer many of the Aberdeen EB-5 Visa questions.

To set the stage for this epic battle on the wide-open prairies with the beautiful skies, here are your advertising rates for South Dakota.

You can purchase a 30-second commercial on the big news talk radio station out of Sioux Falls for less than $30 per spot. You can purchase a 30- second commercial on cable television (covering a hundred channels) in South Dakota for about the same or not much more. This includes Fox News for the entire state. Keep in mind, you have only two cities in South Dakota that have television stations. Now imagine what you can do with a quarter of a million dollars with those sorts of ad rates? You can literally carpet bomb the entire state with campaign commercials for months on end.

The candidates are ready, the management teams are ready, the talking points are ready, but little did I know what was coming next. It would rock my world to the core.

PIZZA RANCHES AND RUBBER CHICKENS, OH MY!

The first thing a coach or a manager of a new team wants to determine is, "*Where are the players at, in regard to their skill levels?*" Probably the most famous instance of this occurred in January of 1959 when the Green Bay Packers hired a man who would become the most legendary coach in the history of the National Football League.

That month and year brought Vince Lombardi to the frozen tundra of Lambeau Field. As the grizzly coach entered the locker room for his first team meeting, he held up a football and announced, "This is a football," much to his team's dismay. With that simple pronouncement, he actually made two bold statements: first, '*You have been doing everything wrong*', and second, '*We are going back to basics boys*'.

Lombardi went on to take his beloved Packers to World Championship after World Championship, dominate the NFL for the next six-plus years, and become one of the winningest sports franchises in all of sports history.

Such was my strategy for our young Senate candidate, Jason

Ravnsborg. When he first inquired as to what I wanted to do and how I wanted to do it, I responded, "I want to watch you interact with voters and listen to you speak." We then discussed more precise messaging.

Shortly after this meeting, Jason had us trekking off to our first campaign event, a meeting of a county Republican Party at a Pizza Ranch. Being from Iowa, I was, of course, familiar with the franchise, which became famous during the 2012 presidential campaign. Senator Rick Santorum kept making references as to how he had won the Iowa Caucuses against all polling, all pundits, and the world's predictions.

When asked by the media how he had won Iowa, he responded, "*I hired Iowa grassroots guru Chuck Laudner and I visited every Pizza Ranch in the state.*"

Basically, Pizza Ranch offers a variety of pizzas made to order, but they go a step further with a buffet that includes delicious fried chicken, homemade macaroni and cheese, fresh vegetables, and a salad bar. The average price for this all-you-can-eat extravaganza is less than $10. Located in predominantly conservative states populated with thrifty people, Pizza Ranches are extremely popular. Combine the right pricing with the "*free meeting room*" they give candidates and it's no wonder Pizza Ranch is an attractive meeting place.

In spite of being an Iowa resident, that was my first lunch at the popular restaurant, if you can believe it. When we walked in, Jason immediately began shaking hands with the 20 or 25 Republican faithful assembled. "So far, so good," I thought. Although he was the only candidate present, other speakers included the county chairperson, the county treasurer, and several other officials.

As directed, we all dined first before the speeches began. I quickly briefed Jason on his message while we trudged through the party business. When it was his turn, he stood up and did a tremendous job for my first viewing. He gave a brief resume, told the audience about his service to our nation, promised to vote to strike down funding for Obamacare, and overall gave a great 10-minute presentation. I did critique his presentation for clarity, strength of voice, and authoritative leadership.

And so it went for the next few days. Sometimes we would drive 20 miles from the hotel to another "grip and grin;" other times we drove hundreds of miles. It has been my first request for the campaign to rent an SUV (preferably black), a four-wheel drive. Keep in mind, it was still technically winter and we were in South Dakota – a state that has been known to have full-blown blizzards in May.

Then came our first Lincoln Day Dinner. For those who are not familiar with them, Lincoln Day Dinners are usually an annual affair, held for the purpose of fundraising. The cost of admission can range from $25 up to $100 depending on if it's a statewide event or a local county event. It turns out, *every county* in South Dakota holds a Lincoln Day Dinner.

While the local meetings were usually held at a Pizza Ranch or a local café backroom, the Lincoln Dinners were usually held at hotel banquet rooms, with the exception of Rapid City and Sioux Falls. These had to be held at much larger venues because of the bigger turnouts.

My first Lincoln Day Dinner marked the first chance I'd had to meet the other candidates in a face-to-face setting. For the most part, they were friendly and expressed curiosity about my presence there. After I had informed them of my position with Jason, they smiled, nodded, and walked off – well, all of them *except* Stace Nelson.

Stace and I actually shared somewhat of a bond for several reasons. The first being that he was a Tea Party candidate who was preaching Tea Party values on the stump. The second was that he was part of the brotherly camaraderie from both of us being veterans. He is a proud Marine and I am a proud Navy veteran. I say he "is" a proud Marine even though he was retired. I learned this lesson the hard way.

Once years ago, I happened to be in a truck-stop in Atlanta, Georgia. I was sitting at the counter with a fellow who happened to be wearing a ball cap that said *United States Marines* on the front. I made the mistake of asking this burly looking truck driver, "Oh are you an ex-Marine?"

Big mistake, I learned.

He stood up and kept on standing up, and up some more until he'd fully risen to a height of at least 6-feet, 8-inches, if not taller. He weighed probably 350 pounds with what appeared to be zero body fat. Had he been 20 years younger, this fellow would have been paid unlimited amounts of money by the Chicago Bears to protect their quarterback.

As he strode around the counter, I think I saw my life flash before my eyes. He approached me, laid the largest hand I have ever seen on my shoulder and proceeded to explain, "There are no ex-Marines, there are only live Marines and dead Marines." Choking back my inner self's compulsion to scream, *Help!*, I simply nodded and said, "Yes, Marine." He smiled and returned to his seat, explaining that the Marine Corps was a brotherhood you earn; once you earn the title Marine, after graduating boot camp, it stays with you for the rest of your life.

By applying this level of respect toward Stace, I believe I scored immediate brownie points with this rather large Marine. I don't know what it is about members of this branch of the military, but they all seem to be gargantuan fellows. At 6-feet, 4-inches, Stace weighed somewhere between 280-300 pounds and his hands were literally twice the size of mine.

As we chatted for a few minutes and reminisced about our military years, he then asked me the $64 question. "So Ken, what brings you to South Dakota?" Again, I gave my stock answer. His response floored me.

"Ken, you do know that Jason Ravnsborg is in this race to be a ringer and he doesn't actually want to win the Senate seat, don't you?"

Stace then went on to explain that Jason was a plant to grab some Tea Party votes in order that Mike Rounds (the former Governor) was assured a victory in the primary without having to go through a runoff election. His payoff would be that the "establishment" would back him for the Attorney General gig in the next election; Jason was merely paying his dues to the Republican Party of South Dakota. This newest revelation hit me like a ton of bricks.

Was it true? Was it just rumor? South Dakota? My beloved adopted state I'd placed so much faith in as being homespun, with those impeccably honest cowboy values?

I honestly did not know how to respond to these allegations. All I could say was, "How do you know?" Stace then launched into an extremely detailed explanation of names I had never heard of, including some who were former college buddies with the dashing young candidate. At the end of his dissertation, Stace basically challenged me to prove him wrong about his theory of why Jason was in this race. I excused myself, exited the conversation, and returned to my appointed seat next to Jason for my rubber chicken Lincoln Day supper, preparing to listen to a multitude of speeches.

However, I wasn't yet ready to challenge my candidate about this possible plot twist in the campaign; at least not yet. I needed some sort of proof.

As the Lincoln Day Dinners dragged on, along with the Pizza Ranch buffet lunches, I had truly reached the point where I didn't want to ever see another chicken breast or a slice of pizza ever again.

With every speech, Jason became more polished and smoother in his delivery, and more adept at visiting, listening and befriending voters. He was still a little uncomfortable in his skin, but he was rapidly becoming a formidable candidate.

The first debate has been set. Sponsored by the state's largest newspaper, it was held at the State Capital in Pierre, South Dakota. In the days leading up to the event, we'd attended countless dinners and *grip and grins* at Pizza Ranches and coffee shops. In the midst of all of this activity, we naturally bumped into other candidates. Once again, Stace Nelson brought up the subject of Jason's bogus campaign.

Apparently, he was a bit concerned about Jason pulling votes from his campaign, due to my presence and my endorsement of Jason for Senate. Furthermore, Jason was also a decorated veteran and up until now, Stace had been the logical choice for the veteran vote in South Dakota.

As if Stace Nelson wasn't enough to give me pause, now I had one of the candidates running for Governor broaching the same subject with me. Lora Hubbell, who was contesting sitting Governor Dennis Daugaard, also informed me about Jason's questionable candidacy (albeit with a little more tact). Sadly, they were not alone: several other candidates for various high-ranking state positions shared the exact same accusations. Many of them included a slight twist or turn in the story, but the bottom line was that Jason had in fact taken a deal from the Mike Rounds campaign to dilute the votes of the most conservative factions of the party from Rhoden, Nelson, and the good doctor. These were the charges leveled against him. However, at this point, I had multiple allegations, but no solid proof.

I had decided that the debate in Pierre would be a perfect opportunity for Jason to bring up the topic of the EB-5 scandal live and on the air in front of the entire state. We had been through all the normal topics and I felt Jason was ready. But when I threw in the monkey-wrench about EB-5 (this scandal at the time was actually under investigation by the government if memory serves me correctly), my candidate balked.

Why would he balk at blasting the front-runner with the biggest scandal to hit the state in 100 years, particularly when every paper in the state was saying the same thing?

That accusation being that Governor Mike Rounds was responsible for massive amounts of missing cash, a scandal involving work visas, and a dead body that met its demise under highly suspicious circumstances.

A no-brainer, right? But balk he did!

His reticence on the matter of broaching such an obvious WMD on live, national television was gravely concerning to me. After the debate, during which he performed well, I confronted my candidate again about his refusal to confront the Governor in a strong, forthright manner about these allegations of fraud, waste, and corruption.

His response was pretty simple: *"Ken, we in South Dakota view that sort of thing as dirty campaigning. The voters won't like it if I get down in the mud."*

Now we had a wedge in our campaign. Jason felt as though using the EB-5 scandal was "dirty pool" and I thought it was fair game because it was in all the papers; to me, it was the two-ton elephant in the room. I felt like we should be talking about it because everyone else was talking about it.

Because he was the only one mentioning it, Stace Nelson was left to twist in the wind. Had Jason also jumped on the bandwagon, that would have given Stace a lot more credibility, plus it would have made the issue much more prominent in the campaign. As a result, we all could have forced a run-off election. But my guy would not go within nine miles of it.

Somewhere in May, I had brought in a media expert, a *guru* I knew from Dallas, Texas. This fellow is widely known as a commercial genius for developing brilliant television ads. I had already taken Jason down to several local radio stations to cut ads for the campaign, but truth be told, we were not competitive with Rounds because of our budget versus his budget. He had an enormous amount of cash-on-hand while we did not. That was the bottom line. Nevertheless, we proceeded as planned and once again the subject of EB-5 came up. We could have easily inserted it as the topic in the ad, but Jason would have nothing of it. Still, I pretty much turned Lee loose with the instructions, "Come up with something fabulous."

Boy, did he ever. About three days later, I was walking to my room at the hotel when Lee stuck his head out of his door and cried, "Check this out!"

A fellow by the name of *Bob Jump* did the voiceover. He's the guy with the deep, baritone voice heard on multiple commercials that can sound so sinister. Jason's ad, produced by Lee with a voiceover by Jump, began by showing clippings of headlines from statewide newspapers about EB-5 and a photo of the dead state official (where it said he died mysteriously), all flashing in rapid-fire fashion. The script used Jump's voice as a narrator, saying something along the lines of, "*Mike Rounds, surrounded in scandal; Mike Rounds this and Mike Rounds that.*"

Oh my, it was a work of art. The first half of it also featured grainy, dark images before the light came on and a happy voice began singing the praises of Jason Ravnsborg.

This advertisement was a perfect vehicle for driving Rounds numbers down and forcing that coveted run-off election I knew we could achieve. For the first time in the campaign, I was actually giddy. I knew this commercial would plummet Rounds' poll numbers by 20 points; between Stace pounding him on the issue and our new ad, we had Rounds right where I wanted him.

And yet, Jason vetoed the entire project instantly!

A day or two later, we had an event on the western end of the state, where Jason performed well. However, my mind was so preoccupied with that commercial that the entire drive back I talked incessantly about it to my candidate, peppering him with question after question about the allegations that had been presented to me. This went on for six hours; the longer I spoke, the angrier I became. I could tell that Jason, too, had reached the end of his patience with me and my continued badgering.

The bottom line was, we had worked hard for several months. While Jason had gotten some extremely positive press, it simply was not enough for him to rise in the polling enough to emerge as a viable candidate against the Mike Rounds machine. This ad could have been a game-changer, but Jason still refused to run it on statewide television. His excuse remained the same. "I refuse to be involved in negative campaigning and dirty politics."

I knew in my heart that this was the end and these allegations were true. It was the only logical answer. That's when I told him, *"Jason, you say you want to be a United States Senator; you have invested an enormous amount of money on your efforts and I am handing this to you. I am literally handing you a runoff election I know you can win and you refuse to take it. Are these allegations true?"*

He would not answer the question. And that *was* my answer.

In retrospect, I don't blame Jason for handling his campaign the way he did. For me, it was frustrating because I had invested incalculable hours (and sleepless nights) working on it. In terms of Senate candidates, Jason was young. In order to win this election, he would have had to literally pee on the Republican Party and its boss in a state in which he lived and practiced law.

If the allegations are true, it means the party hierarchy came to Jason and made him an offer he couldn't refuse: *"Behave yourself, take one for the team, and we will take care of you down the road."* And I truly believe that is what happened. It shattered my idyllic image of the state of South Dakota but reminded me why the Tea Party exists. It has had enough of party cronyism, which is why we want and need to turn the party upside down and start over.

EIGHTEEN

ARE WE DOOMED TO REPEAT HISTORY?

We began this saga of the *Modern Great American Tea Party* movement by rising up against wasteful government spending, high taxes, bailouts of "too rich to fail" banks, and for the most part, economic issues.

Because of the conservative nature of the movement and the fact that it grew so rapidly, the Tea Party became sort of pseudo big tent for conservatism across the board. It welcomed with open-arms Second Amendment coalitions, pro-life coalitions, homeschoolers (a.k.a., anti-government education advocates), and Christian groups of all shapes, sizes, and denominations.

The benefit in the early power of the Tea Party was that most, if not all of the voting base were comprised of registered Republicans. As time went on, frustration with the GOP increased, along with the masses. Many within the movement flipped their registrations from Republican to Independent.

Early on in the initial rise to prominence of the Tea Party, patriots could see something significant happening. They could actually attend a rally, where they could commiserate with fellow like-minded thinkers, pitch their political philosophy, and, for a lack of better description, participate in an event akin to an AA meeting. Fellow citizens knew and understood your perspective and you bonded with the like-minded.

This was clearly evident in the mass upsets of 2010. The Tea Party had coalesced to some degree, which resulted in the masses showing up at the polls to vote for conservative candidates, thus giving the GOP a majority in the House of Representatives. In fact, the win was so large, it now holds the record as the largest swing from one party to another party in American history. With the flipping of 60-something seats in one election, it was utterly astounding.

Then came 2012.

While the Tea Party was still intact for the most part, the passion had begun to wane as the larger groups kept growing and scooping up money. By now, the huge rallies were no longer taking place.

What was the problem?

The base of the Republican Party did not see results. Emails from the big groups went out almost daily to the Tea Party faithful, advising them of the shenanigans of House Speaker John Boehner, along with pitches of "donate now" to save this or fight that. Yet, in the end, Boehner did what he wanted to do. Simply put, the grassroots were frustrated by the tone-deafness of their own leaders. Simultaneously, the voter registration cards kept being filled in as "Independent." Now we began to witness fracturing, not just within the Republican Party, but within the Tea Party as well.

As the 2012 cycle drew closer, I remember receiving many emails from patriots with questions about the various candidates. One constant, common theme amongst all of them was, "Who is the Tea Party supporting for the 2012 primary season?"

Personally speaking, my response was, "In Iowa I will support

Congresswoman Bachmann because she is indisputably the most politically conservative in the race."

Of course, we now know what happened. Due to Bachmann's internal campaign chaos, combined with a few missteps and the religious right in Iowa, she lost to Senator Rick Santorum. Keep in mind, Santorum was not the most politically conservative, he was the most religiously conservative.

The Iowa Caucuses in 2012 were the first indication that the Christian right had made huge inroads into what had begun as the TEA (Taxed Enough Already) PARTY – and was now becoming a hodgepodge of conservatism across the board. In other words, the fighters for liberty, tax, and economic sanity were being replaced by ministers and folks for social conservatism.

One might reasonably ask, "So what's the problem?"

My answer is that the religious right only votes ideological principles.

Earlier I explained what happened to Governor Mitt Romney, who won the nomination and lost an election that my blind dog could have pulled off. Obama's approval numbers were literally in the sewer. He'd already racked up staggering debt, left an Embassy in Benghazi smoldering, and enacted policies that helped put millions upon millions out of work. This election should have been a landslide for Romney. Instead, countless millions sat it out because Mitt Romney did not meet the Christian purity test.

The excuses by my brethren on the right ranged from, "Romney had written Obamacare and even had a $50 co-pay for abortions in Massachusetts," to "Romney is a Mormon and Mormonism is a cult." Then there was, "Romney is too rich and doesn't understand the middle-class at all," and my all-time favorite, "Romney is a RINO and should be a registered Democrat, plus he is the establishment pick and we cannot support the establishment pick."

This rigid mindset left Governor Mitt Romney doomed from the beginning; he just didn't know it until it was too late.

I find the treatment the Tea Party gave Romney nothing short of hypocritical. The movement claims to support constitutional principles, and to a large degree, they do. Yet, Mitt Romney went through the constitutional process to win the nomination. Millions of citizens voted in those primaries but the Tea Party refused to support the votes cast by fellow Americans. They simply thought they knew better and the American people had selected the wrong candidate; or worse yet, the evil "Establishment" had selected the nominee for them.

When the smoke cleared on Election Night 2012, Barack Obama had won re-election by some 3 million votes. Had the Tea Party gone to their polling locations en masse instead of sitting it out, Romney would have won that election by at least 20 million votes, which would have more than covered Ohio, Pennsylvania, Florida, and many other states to give Romney the electoral college win.

Now the question becomes: *Are we doomed to repeat 2012 in future elections?*

YES, is the answer!

The fact is, without properly organizing this gigantic herd of cats (who seem to be straying) we will no doubt repeat 2012 over and over again. In fact, we are already seeing the lines being drawn in the sand for 2016.

In Iowa for instance, we once again had Bob Vander Platts, radio announcer Steve Deace, and more religious leaders supporting Senator Ted Cruz. Normally this would not be a problem, except, the reasoning given for their support is that Ted is the most religiously right and principled in his Christian values.

The one item these people seem to forget is, we are not electing an American Pastor or American Pope; we are electing a President.

While it is nice having a President that respects Christian values, it is not a constitutional prerequisite that our President is a Baptist or Methodist or any other mainstream Christian religion. The fact is, had the Tea Party put this religious prerequisite aside and supported the last nominee, we would not have the object of their disdain currently occupying the White House today.

But this was not to be. The very book the Tea Party claims to believe in features multiple passages about ego and arrogance, and how they will be our downfall. The problem with the movement at present is their extreme arrogance. Most members feel they are superior to the average American because of patriotism. *"I wave a Gadsden flag, I say the Pledge of Allegiance and I spew patriotic rhetoric; therefore I am a patriot and my opinion of our nation holds more value than yours does."*

A classic example of this is the Tea Party's stance on gay marriage. Many recent rallies and protests have been organized for the purpose of opposing same-sex marriage. *Remember, the Tea Party stands for Constitutional principles, right?* Most, if not all the states that have legalized this practice have done so because their Supreme Court has ruled on it and said, *"There is nothing in the Constitution that addresses this issue;"* therefore, they have to approve it based on personal liberty.

This one issue has further split the Republican Party from the Tea Party. My argument has been, *"So when do we stand for the Constitution?"* The Supreme Court of Iowa ruled! The Supreme Court of the United States ruled! Every Supreme Court has ruled against the religious factions of the Tea Party, so why are we still fighting about this?

Arrogance and faux self-righteousness are the reasons.

Once again, we believe that only we have the keys to patriotism and the right to preach to the masses.

The stand that the Tea Party takes on the issue of gay marriage is but one in a long list that many politicians want to run from at all costs. Gay marriage, for instance, is supported by some 60% of the American people. It is a no-win issue for candidates to campaign on, except for Tea Party candidates.

Tea Party candidates and their millions of supporters and followers also pay special attention to abortion. The truth is, the issue had been settled at the Supreme Court level on January 22, 1973, with the Roe versus Wade ruling. Yet, the Tea Party forces candidates to state their position on the right to life. Mitt Romney, for instance, was pro-life in his campaign position and speeches, yet the Tea Party punished him beyond belief because of his state's health-care plan because it had a $50 co-pay provision for their indigent policyholders.

To me, this is insanity. We are punishing Congressional candidates who can actually win an election and install another conservative as a Supreme Court Justice. A member of the House of Representatives can sit in that seat for the next 20 years and will never be asked to vote on the subject of abortion, yet this is one of the Tea Party's fitness tests for their candidacy. Of course, if candidates capitulate to the Tea Party, then they lose votes across the board from the rest of the party, or if the candidate is a little more moderate, they lose Democrat voters as well.

One of the principle groups behind the Tea Party's meteoric rise in popularity was the group funded by the Koch Brothers, Americans For Prosperity (AFP). AFP has helped to fund many major rallies across America and their principle angle with respect to the Tea Party movement is "free markets." For the record, I too believe in free markets, but I also believe prudence should be the first rule.

So why are the billionaire brothers so interested in free markets?

I'm not going to pick on the Koch Brothers specifically because if the truth is known, nobody knows all of the inner workings of their massive holdings. What I am prepared to say that is that folks like the

Koch Brothers have preached this *free market mantra* for years.

Today in America, we have nearly 100 million citizens who have either given up on finding work, are looking for work, or are underemployed with part-time, instead of full-time, hours. A big part of the reason for this unfortunate and unnecessary predicament is that these groups had trade and tax laws changed through expensive lobbying efforts. Today, corporations relocate overseas and do so with tax benefits, cheaper labor costs, no import duties, and much higher corporate profit margins.

The fallout from this has been that millions upon millions of jobs have been sent to foreign lands, most of them under the banner of "free markets." While I do agree with the concept of free markets, the American worker must be protected at all costs.

While the Tea Party overall has been good for America, it has certainly had and is still undergoing severe growing pains. The average Tea Party member simply wants to have their voice heard on Capitol Hill. The average member wants our enormous waste curtailed, spending cut back to far more reasonable amounts, lost liberties restored, and a return of sanity to our government. They want the federal government to relinquish control back to the states on several matters, such as education.

Currently within the Tea Party, if you are holding a meeting at a local group and 50 members are present, you will get 45 different answers on what needs to be done. Some of the answers are moderate in nature while others are off the charts to the right. I have actually heard Tea Party members state categorically that '*there is nothing in the constitution about Social Security, we need to cut that out of our budget.*'

With watching what is currently transpiring in this election cycle of 2016, it is very troubling to see so many who are willing to once again sit out in a juvenile protest based upon moralistic values. The fact is America, we as a nation are in a deep, deep hole. We are now officially on the road to $20 trillion in debt. According to most of our top economists (in fact over 100 have chimed in on this topic) including a Nobel Prize winner, once we hit the magic number of $24 trillion, we are economically collapsing as a nation.

This one topic alone is beyond frightening because most experts in this field all agree that if our dollar collapses, we will descend into what would be nothing less than a full-scale revolution.

When you have tens of millions of armed, hungry, and angry citizens looking for food, there is no controlling the situation. We could almost without a doubt expect our nation's capital to be burned to the ground. It would then be anyone's guess as to what happens next. And once again, we are at the point where evangelicals are supporting one candidate who it appears will not win the nomination. Ted Cruz will most likely not win the nomination, but what happens if he doesn't? Does the Tea Party stay home again because they won't support Marco Rubio or Donald Trump?

This is exactly what is shaping up to be the case. Once again, the object of the Tea Party's disdain will be elected if the Tea Party stays home on Election Day.

America, we are talking about 40-50 million voters here. This is not a small faction with an attitude. This is a full blown army that is willing to sit out and throw an election.

NINETEEN

WHERE DO WE GO FROM HERE?

There is little doubt that America's modern day Tea Party faithful are the most passionate, vocal political devotees in our nation today. These folks are on the front lines of every major and not-so-major political event affecting our great land.

Whether it is an immigration rally opposing amnesty, a Second Amendment event defending our precious constitutional rights, a protest against high taxes and in favor of tax reform, or a pushback against a RINO House Speaker for his stupid liberal appeasement, the faithful show up. They come in the rain, the heat, the wind, the snow, or sub-zero temperatures. Nothing stops these dedicated patriots from expressing their love or frustration to our elected officials.

They rally in D.C., San Mateo, Denver, Billings, Madison, Orlando, Fort Worth, Garland, Kansas City and Des Moines. They rally in Hartford, Roanoke, Nashville, and Little Rock. All across our fruited plain, they come, they work, they volunteer, and they express their undying devotion to this great experiment known as the United States of America.

Why is it then, if multitudes of Tea Party citizens show up, rally, and vote in droves, moderate 'RINO's' or worse yet, Barack Obama, get re-elected? In one word: disorganization. It's simply an abject lack of leadership.

The Republican Party establishment's greatest fear is if the Tea Party ever manages to get its act together and become an organized force. If that happens, the Republican hierarchy will be pulling their hair out and having a nervous breakdown.

Basically, what you have with the Tea Party are the "old-guard" Republicans, some conservative John F. Kennedy Democrats, and a whole trainload of Constitutional-adhering conservatives.

When the Democrat Party went off the rails and nominated a Marxist-Socialist with Barack Obama, the party swung way out into left field. This forced the Republican Party to the left (hence the term RINO), which in turn, left millions upon millions of disgruntled Barry Goldwater and Ronald Reagan types without a home – until the rise of the Tea Party. It is not a voting bloc to be trifled with, and that is exactly what the Republican operatives of the world are doing. The GOP expects this group to vote because they falsely believe they will automatically fall in line and support the "electable" party candidate for any office, purely because he or she is better than a Democrat.

Wrong!

These people are extremely principled voters who will refuse to show up because a.) They believe it's the best way to show their dissatisfaction; and b.) They won't compromise their vote for someone they don't believe in.

So, what now? Where do we go from here and how do we get all these beloved patriots on one page and pointed in one powerful direction?

Judge Reed A. Chambers II has the answer.

THE U.S. TEA PARTY LOYALISTS NATIONAL TEA PARTY MOVEMENT BATTLE PLAN

The US Tea Party Loyalists "NATIONAL TEA PARTY MOVEMENT BATTLE PLAN" is that the Tea Party is a conservative "pressure group" and not a new political party. Our decentralized Battle Plan for conservative Republicans is to be a phalanx of grassroots *Reagan Revolution* voters, as a "build it and they will come" effort, in order to be far better organized to effectively influence elections.

National out-of-state tea parties MUST NOT select a congressional, state, or local candidate; such decisions are for state resident tea party members to make. Our unique plan is to act as an umbrella group for mutual meetings with independent tea party groups, all local area tea parties of the Tea Party Patriots, Tea Party Express, or Tea Party Loyalists, and "affinity" tea parties (a common activity or interests - The US Tea Party Loyalists 2nd Amendment Caucus, US Tea Party Loyalists Right to Life Caucus, US Tea Party Loyalists State and Federal Tax Lid Caucus, etc.) Locality and affinity tea party groups conduct regular meetings every other week, with quarterly joint mass meetings of county conventions, congressional district caucuses, and semiannual state conferences. We will also hold an annual Tea Party National Assembly.

Tea party county conventions send three proposed State Laws, and the congressional district caucuses propose three Federal Laws. State Conferences select TEN MOST WANTED STATE LAWS, and the TEN MOST WANTED FEDERAL LAWS, for each state and federal Representative and Senator. If state or federal legislators vote for all ten of the most wanted laws, they get a 100% State Tea Party rating (legislative sponsors and co-sponsors of a Ten Most Wanted Law gives that legislator a bonus 5% Tea Party Rating for each such Bill sponsored or cosponsored). But any state or federal legislator gleaning a 70% or lower State Tea Party Rating will get a Tea Party opponent from the US Tea Party Candidate's Prep School in the next primary election, to replace an unworthy incumbent who has failed to be loyal to their own state tea party's Ten Most Wanted Laws list.

Congressional District Caucuses elect one Delegate, and each of the 50 State Conferences elects two delegates, to the US Tea Party Political Activists Electoral College. All Tea Party Incumbent public servants and tea party national organization officers are ex-officio "Super Delegates." The 535 Tea Party Delegates and Super Delegates meet before the Iowa presidential caucuses, in a NATIONAL TEA PARTY MOVEMENT PRESIDENTIAL PREFERENCE CONVENTION, immediately before actual state-by-state caucuses or primary election voting occurs for choosing delegates to the GOP National Convention. Candidates participating in the NATIONAL TEA PARTY MOVEMENT PRESIDENTIAL PREFERENCE CONVENTION voting speak to the US Tea Party Electoral College, which is an "earned media" news event that C-Span will be invited to show "gavel to gavel" national TV coverage.

The NATIONAL TEA PARTY MOVEMENT PRESIDENTIAL PREFERENCE CONVENTION endorses one candidate as the US Tea Party GOP US Presidential candidate and also a Vice President of the United States endorsed Tea Party Candidate.

A separately conducted Tea Party National Assembly makes no Presidential or Vice Presidential endorsements but does conduct a straw poll and also identifies The National Tea Party Movement's TEN MOST CRITICALLY NEEDED FEDERAL LAWS, each of which is taken from the 500 Most Wanted Federal Laws that were adopted from the 50 Tea Party State Conferences. The opposition of even ONE of the NATIONAL TEA PARTY MOVEMENT'S TEN MOST CRITICALLY NEEDED FEDERAL LAWS will incur Censure and a Proclamation of the Chair of the Tea Party National Assembly to expel a member of Congress from the GOP.

Do you think that the electorate is bone-weary of lying politicians who say one thing during a campaign and then when elected, fail to do what they promised to do on the campaign trail? The National Tea Party Movement will, on a state-by-state basis, by the initiative of new laws by the submission of written petitions, seek to amend election laws at statewide initiative elections. FIRST: to authorize electoral opponents to send to each other, Notice of Video Depositions to be taken, Written Interrogatories, Demands for the Production of Documents and other things, all of which shall be proffered under notarized oath or affirmation, under the penalties of perjury.

A candidate's refusal to comply with STATE ELECTORAL DISCOVERY LAWS would lead to that candidate being dropped from the ballot in that state, and his or her name being barred from obtaining any state certification of the results of an election; and, SECOND, a state election law initiative that would permit two thousand five hundred or more political party members who have voted in three or more previous primary elections of the affected political party, to sign a petition to place any candidate or incumbent's name on the next occurring state party primary election ballot, at the bottom of all candidate's names, the YES or NO ballot question:

"Shall (candidate or incumbent's name) be expelled from this political party and as a consequence of being expelled, shall such any expelled person also be banned from all future elections (or subsequent caucuses) to be conducted in this state, as a candidate to any public office of the (Republican)(Democrat) Party of this state?"

In this manner, any incumbent whose voting record is offensive to his or her party's base voters, may be disciplined by the rank and file state political party members voting in a future primary election, to by a majority vote of all votes cast on the question, expel a disloyal political party member in that state and ban the expelled person from ever being an endorsed candidate of that political party ever again. RINOs take note. We are FED UP with being told one thing by candidates before they are elected, only to see them abandon their campaign promises and vote the opposite of what they promised WE THE PEOPLE after they have been elected.

The National Tea Party Battle Plan also includes the appointment of Political District or State and County Coordinators, Block Captains, and also Precinct Workers, to do door-to-door canvassing and to attend to elections in like manner as do Union members, to pass issue and candidates' campaign literature, serve hot and cold drinks, and offer voters an opportunity to sign-in and to participate in Exit Polls, at TEA PARTY NEIGHBOR'S TABLES. These tables will be arranged close to where voters park their cars prior to casting their votes. Tea Party Poll Workers will all wear identifying clothing and campaign hats.

Sincerely and respectfully submitted,

Judge Reed A. Chambers II
State Administrative Judge, Retired.
National Executive Director
US Tea Party Loyalists

Judge Reed's plan is a much more detailed version of my own **Blue Print**, which I've laid out below.

Organization:

Someone needs to form one blanket organization with a broad nameplate, i.e., *The American Tea Party* or something similar. It will have to be someone with some deep pockets who is willing to truly invest in America and believes deeply in constitutional conservatism.

The organization will need to be set up with 50 state offices and a national headquarters. Each office needs a state director and a staff to direct major events, and rallies, and keep track of candidates who are running for State Representative and Senate seats, House Seats, U. S. Senate seats and, of course, Presidential seats.

The purpose of these state offices is also to direct ground forces to help "our" candidates get elected. These offices will VET candidates (after the vetting forms are written and approved by the national office and Board of Directors).

Example:

The candidate for the U.S. House of Representatives is vetted, then approved, which means he or she will have the full support of ATP (American Tea Party). This support includes a built-in volunteer base and funding from the ATP as well as ATP's national Political Action Committee, which will run advertising on behalf of that candidate and against their opponent. The blueprint remains the same for all political races at the local, state, and national levels.

A further example of the amount of devastation this could cause for the all mainstream parties would be Orlando, Florida. A few years ago, the Orlando Tea Party had over 50,000 members on its rolls. Could you imagine 5,000 of these folks working every weekend in the House district for whomever we wanted to be Congressman in Orlando? We would never again lose that race to a Democrat or an RINO!

The big problem comes with the presidential race as we are witnessing now and we lived through back in 2012. The solution? We simply hold a convention just as the Democrats and Republicans do.

However.

Our convention's purpose is NOT to run a "Third-Party" candidate, which would accomplish nothing, other than to guarantee a victory for the Democrats/Socialists. What we would want to do here would be to hold state conventions every election cycle. Conduct the business of deciding who we want to support, then elect delegates for each state. It would need to be determined how many Tea Party groups from each state would participate to organize our beginning American Tea Party after a mass marketing and advertising campaign has been conducted.

The reason for this is, current Tea Party groups like Tea Party Patriots are most likely not going to give us their membership roster to contact because we would be stripping their fundraising away. Remember, they have been earning millions upon millions for all these years, and they aren't just going to give it up. Therefore, we need to start a major national push to bring their members over to the national organization known as ATP.

Once this happens, we assign delegates to each state. When the national convention happens (which should probably be annual to conduct business) those delegates attend the national convention. They are the rule makers; the leadership for ATP.

When our presidential cycle comes along, the delegates then select who they want to support. *The key here is, the millions of members of ATP all agree to support who the delegates have chosen to back for President.* The convention literally brings in the candidates who have announced just prior to the Iowa Caucuses, to address the convention and do their best to sell themselves to ATP. This is done *prior* to Iowa, in order that we can assist our chosen candidate in The Hawkeye State to start them off with a win right out of the box. Remember those ground troops and volunteers? This is what they are for. *Ground Game!*

With some 600 Tea Party groups across America currently, there is zero reason why this idea couldn't be implemented. With over 15 to 20,000,000 registered members, plus twice that many who vote with the Tea Party, it is highly likely that with a good marketing effort, we could put 25-30 million on the rosters and form the largest lobbying effort in American history; one that is organized to carry the banner of conservatism forward in America.

Again, the problem is the current leadership of the large Tea Parties currently in existence. They will do whatever is necessary to prevent the above plan from working. They know that if something like this were to succeed, then their gravy train is over. They know this would put their organization out of business. I have no doubt my book will be derided as a piece of rubbish. Although many will say it is chock full of lies, nothing could be further from the truth. Every word in this book *is* the truth.

Simply ask yourselves this question: If all those millions

upon millions raised were utilized, where are the results? Why do substandard candidates keep running and losing? Why aren't the good candidates being supported? What expenses are so costly that it takes tens of millions a year to operate a Tea Party that has very few, if any, expenses in comparison to the amount of money raised and spent on election cycles?

I am not charging anything; I am merely asking questions. I would love some answers. But after eight years of Tea Party rallies and tens of millions donated to Tea Party organizations, we are no further down the road than we were nearly a decade ago. It is time for some closet cleaning. It is time to get this ship pointed in the right direction, and it is time to take our country back from the Marxists, Socialists, Liberals, Political Correctness Nazis, and all others who don't want to contribute, but just criticize and take from our nation. It is time to install servants who actually want to serve our nation rather than enrich themselves before relocating to Fiji with a large bank account.

America is broken. But America has an enormous band of brothers and sisters who love her, have served her, and are willing to keep serving her. We just need to clean our own closets; then we can begin cleaning up our nation's mess.

God bless you and thank you for taking the time to read my book.

REFERENCES

1. Heritage Foundation: *Homeschooling Sees Dramatic Rise in Popularity*, Lindsay Burke, 2009.
   http://www.heritage.org/research/reports/2009/01/homeschooling-sees-dramatic-rise-in-popularity

2. Houston Chronicle Poll on Americans' Support for Religious Freedom, December 31, 2015
   http://www.chron.com/news/nation-world/article/Poll-American-support-for-religious-freedom-6730012.php

3. Houston Chronicle Poll: *nearly 80% of Americans say they are Christian*, January 5, 2012.
   http://www.chron.com/life/houston-belief/article/Poll-Nearly-80-percent-of-Americans-say-they-are-2444092.php

4. Gandhi, film/drama, 1982.
   http://www.amazon.com/Gandhi-Ben-Kingsley/dp/B00190N4E4

5. Washington Times, *Obama Secretly Backing Muslim Brotherhood*, Bill Gertz, June 3, 2015.
   http://www.washingtontimes.com/news/2015/jun/3/inside-the-ring-muslim-brotherhood-has-obamas-secr/?page=all

6. Shoebat.com, *Obama Administration Officials Who Are Muslim And Who Are Linked to Muslim Brotherhood Fail To Make List of 20 Officials Benghazi Committee Chairman Wants to Interview*, Ben Barrack, February 7, 2015.
   http://shoebat.com/2015/02/07/obama-administration-officials-muslim-linked-muslim-brotherhood-fail-make-list-20-officials-benghazi-committee-chairman-wants-interview/

7. CNN.com, *Palin Opens Tea Party Protest in Reid's Hometown*, March 30, 2010
   http://www.cnn.com/2010/POLITICS/03/27/reid.tea.party/

8. ReviewJournal.com, *Thousands gather for Tea Party Express Event in Reid's Hometown*, March 27, 2010
   http://www.reviewjournal.com/news/thousands-gather-tea-party-express-event-harry- reids-hometown

9. New York Times, *Palin Rallies Tea Party Crowd in Nevada*, Kate Zernike,

March 27, 2010
http://www.nytimes.com/2010/03/28/us/politics/28nevadaweb.html?_r=0

10. The Iowa Republican, *Controversial Crow Departs Tea Party Group*, Kevin Hall, November 14, 20111.
http://www.theiowarepublican.com/2011/controversial-crow-departs-tea-party-group/

11. CNN.com, *Iowa Tea Party group cancels O'Donnell Speaking Appearance.*
http://www.cnn.com/2011/POLITICS/08/30/tea.party.odonnell/

12. HotAir.com, *Blame the organizers for the snafu at the tea-party rally, not Palin,* Allahpundit, August 31, 2011.
http://hotair.com/archives/2011/08/31/blame-the-organizers-for-the-snafu-at-the-iowa-tea-party-rally-not-palin/

13. TheSpeechATimeForChoosing.Wordpress.com, *Endorsement Power! Sarah Palin: 75% Success Karl Rove: $100 of Millions Spent, Only 1% Success,* Gary P. Jackson, November 12, 2012
https://thespeechatimeforchoosing.wordpress.com/2012/11/12/endorsement-power-sarah-palin-75-success-karl-rove-100s-of-millions-spent-only-1-success/

14. The Daily Beast, *The Mama Grizzly Scorecard, Shushannah Washe,* November 2, 2010.
http://www.thedailybeast.com/articles/2010/11/03/the-2010-midterm-elections-how-did-sarah-palin-and-the-mama-grizzlies-do.html

15. Huffington Post, *Tea Party Comedian Eric Golub Compares Trig Palin to 'Special Needs' Liberals,* May 31, 2012.
http://www.huffingtonpost.com/2011/09/06/tea-party-comedian-compares-liberals-to-trig-palin_n_950570.html

16. CNN.com, *Boiling Point: Key Players,* October 27, 2010
http://www.cnn.com/2010/POLITICS/10/27/key.players/

17. TPM Muckraker, *Tea Party Express' Sal Russo: Mark Williams Is No Longer Affiliated with Our PAC,* Eric Lach, July 20, 2010.
http://talkingpointsmemo.com/muckraker/tea-party-express-sal-russo-mark-williams-is-no-longer-affiliated-with-our-pac

18. FreeRepublic.com, *What is this? Tea Party Express News?* J. Argese, October 5, 2010
http://www.freerepublic.com/focus/bloggers/2602165/posts

19. OpenSecrets.org. - 2014 PAC Summary Data, Our Country Deserves Better PAC/TeaPartyExpress.org

https://www.opensecrets.org/pacs/lookup2.php?strID=C00540898&cycle=2014
https://www.opensecrets.org/pacs/expenditures.
php?cycle=2014&cmte=C00540898

20. Crow's Nest Politics.com, *Hey Tea Party, Time to Declare War on Speaker Paul Ryan*, Ken Crow, December 18, 2015.
http://www.crowsnestpolitics.com/2015/12/18/hey-tea-party-time-to-declare-war-on-speaker-paul-ryan/

21. Argus Leader, *What you need to know about EB-5 in South Dakota*, David Montgomery, October 8, 2014.
http://www.argusleader.com/story/davidmontgomery/2014/10/08/eb-5-primer/16890965/

22. Homeowners Affordability and Stability Plan, HASP https://en.wikipedia.org/wiki/HASP

23. Troubled Asset Relief Program, TARP https://en.wikipedia.org/wiki/Troubled_Asset_Relief_Program

24. Gallup Poll, 60% *of Americans Favor Gay Marriage*: http://www.gallup.com/poll/117328/marriage.aspx

ABOUT THE AUTHOR

Raised with small town values in West Central Texas, Ken Crow was taught at an early age the importance of honesty, integrity and service to the community. These values were further honed with his service to our nation in the U.S. Navy.

Ken has spent most of the last forty years involved in the front lines of politics at one level or another. From his first days as a volunteer for then-candidate Ronald Reagan to managing a United States Senate race in South Dakota, he has been neck-deep in the political arena.

Having been one of the first to be involved in the modern Tea Party, Ken has seen both the good and the corrupt. As one of the original co-founders of the internet sensation, TeaPartyCommunity.com, he has witnessed the positives and the negatives that have arisen from this great American movement. There is nobody more qualified to expose its dark side and elaborate on its positives.

Ken Crow has spoken at local Tea Party events and given stem-winding addresses to major events at State Capitals across America, including the steps of the United States Capitol. He is often called upon to offer political analysis on many national radio shows as well as television news cast.

The beloved father of three lives in Iowa with his loving wife Sonya and two four-legged children who often give political advice as well. Ken is the President of CrowsNestPolitics.com, a nationally recognized conservative website that is often referenced by national and international news and media.

www.ingramcontent.com/pod-product-compliance
Lightning Source LLC
Chambersburg PA
CBHW051741250726
48659CB00001B/181